Endors

My name is Barry Maracle. I am a Mohawk man and a member of the Tyendinaga Mohawk Territory, where I grew up. I learned much of my culture from my Mohawk classes at Quinte Mohawk School, but even more so from my many, many conversations with my grandfather, Karowyakdadeh.

My grandfather's first language was Mohawk and he was beaten every day for speaking Mohawk at the residential school called the Mush-Hole in Brantford, Ontario. I won't share now about his experience except this: "All I know is that I would see my friends one day and then ... I didn't see them anymore."

My grandfather is another story of tragedy to triumph, and I love how Belma has allowed God to use her to bring triumphant stories like this to us! The window that we see through is a panoramic view from many different angles and experiences.

So it is my distinct privilege to endorse my friend Belma Vardy's newest creative collaboration! This woman eats, drinks, and lives honour! I love everything she does!

Not only do I have the honour of endorsing Belma, but I know many of these stories and the people behind them and it is also my privilege to endorse these amazing testimonies! For example, you will hear from Pastor Archi and her sister, Karen Lallean. They talk about their experiences on Walpole Island Reserve with their dad, Wilf Lallean, and how they were taught with the other six siblings to live off the land. Their dad was as amazing as they make him out to be and he also taught me how to skin and stretch muskrats in that same living room! Such a small world. I know the Thunderchilds and the Thomases and many, many others mentioned and have heard these stories as I have traversed this nation.

As you read through this book of so many First People's testimonies, be prepared to be overwhelmed with oceans of irrefutable hope!

This book of raw data compiled in these pages is simply and profoundly the manifestation of the gospel of our Lord Jesus Christ.

You will be led on an emotional roller-coaster ride, going from the depths of horrific tragedy to beautiful moments of transforming lives and communities all across the land we call Turtle Island.

I say all that to say this ...

What God did for all these wonderful people *He will do for you!*

Much love,

—BARRY C. MARACLE
Author of *Wake Up Into Your Dream* (www.barry-maracle.ca)

Belma puts faces to some of the many "children of the soil" of this land. She shares the lives of these overcomers! Several of the stories had even greater meaning and impact for me (Peta-Gay) after having met a few of the people whose stories Belma has shared here. She has a unique perspective of First Nations culture from the inside as a non-Indigenous woman.

Reading Belma's book from a First Nations perspective, we can say, knowing her heart, that she seeks to honour our people with her Native heart and loving disposition.

Belma presents our people as real, modern people of the now, not relics of ancient times, as most history books would have the world believe. This book dispels the myth of the savage Indian and brings life and hope to our people and to anyone who reads it.

It's a must read.

Thank you for sharing hope, Belma!

—DR. GERARD and PETA-GAY ROBERTS
Co-founders of OKAMA (Karina and Taino Nations,
Wumpum carriers of the Grand River Six Nations)

You will be warmed beyond measure as you read the first-hand accounts of First Nations men and women who have been able to share their journeys of rescue from despair, transformation, and vision for their future.

Belma's deep love for these people enables her to passionately and articulately peel back the veneer that covers over the real imprisoning issues that have been in place far too long.

As an old hymn expresses: "The Love of God is greater far than tongue or pen can ever tell. It goes beyond the highest star and reaches to the lowest hell." *Because The Spirit Was There* is a testimony of such enabling, rescuing love.

—MARY AUDREY RAYCROFT
Teaching Pastor, Catch the Fire, Toronto, and founder of
Releasers of Life Equipping Ministry

Over the years I've had the privilege of being impacted by many First Nations people. As a young person, I worked in South Dakota caring for babies on the reservation with dysentery. Years later, I had the honour of meeting and becoming friends with Dr. Jay Swallow and Negiel Bigpond. Jay's account of the Sand Creek Massacre marked me forever. My heart was broken over this gross injustice for and hijacking of the First Nations people. God himself created all of us with value and purpose, calling us out of every tribe, tongue, nation, and people as kings and priests and to become one through God's shed blood. Each of us are created uniquely by God to be carriers of His Presence. We are specifically designed for fulfillment of destiny. Now, Belma's book *Because The Spirit Was There* gives me an even greater insight into God's First Nations people. They are called to be first, the forerunners, leading us into the greatest revival and awakening we've experienced. None of us will thrive the way God intended us to until we honour this great people distinctly designed by

God. Thank you Belma Vardy and Chief Kenny Blacksmith for giving these people a VOICE, including my friends, Arlinda Buckshot and Karen Lallean. As you said, it gives us a window into their real-life stories, ethnic richness, and heritage as well as the knowledge we desperately need to enlarge our hearts and understanding.

—**BARBARA J. YODER**
Founder and lead apostle, Shekinah Christian Church, and author and international speaker

It has been an honour to be part of Belma's first book *Because God Was There*. Both Belma and the Native people have gone through similar tragedies that created great suffering. But God turns suffering into personal growth and blessings. As I read in the pages of this book, *Because The Spirit Was There*, I can testify God did it for my mother and many other natives. These riveting stories will grip your heart as you weave through the tapestry of tragedies filled with pain and sorrow to life-giving open spaces of restoration and healing. It is a delight to see the powerful leading of the Holy Spirit and to witness the impact that this ministry and Belma's books are having among the First Nations people.

—**DR REV. LORNE SHEPHERD**
Metis (part Algonquin, part Iroquois), author, counsellor, speaker

BECAUSE THE SPIRIT WAS THERE

WINDOWS INTO
FIRST NATIONS
COMMUNITIES

FOREWORD BY
CHIEF
KENNY BLACKSMITH

BELMA VARDY

BECAUSE THE SPIRIT WAS THERE
Copyright ©2022 Belma Vardy
978-1-988928-65-4 Soft Cover
978-1-988928-66-1 E-book

Published by Castle Quay Books
Burlington, Ontario, Canada and Jupiter, Florida, U.S.A.
416-573-3249 | info@castlequaybooks.com | www.castlequaybooks.com

Edited by Marina Hofman Willard
Book interior by Burst Impressions
Cover design by Jennifer Gibson www.JenniferGibson.ca

Scripture taken from the Holy Bible, New International Version®, NIV® Copyright ©1973,
1978, 1984, 2011 by Biblica, Inc.® Used by permission. All rights reserved worldwide.

Library and Archives Canada Cataloguing in Publication Coming
Title: Because the Spirit was there : windows into First Nations communities / by Belma
D. Vardy ;
  foreword by Chief Kenny Blacksmith.
Names: Vardy, Belma, author.
Identifiers: Canadiana 20220255334 | ISBN 9781988928654 (softcover)
Subjects: LCSH: Christian biography—Canada. | CSH: First Nations—Canada—
Religion. | CSH: First
  Nations—Canada—Biography. | CSH: First Nations—Violence against—Canada. |
CSH: First Nations—
  Canada—History. | LCGFT: Biographies.
Classification: LCC E98.R3 V37 2022 | DDC 270.089/97071—dc23

CASTLE QUAY BOOKS

Dedication

I dedicate this book to all my Indigenous brothers and sisters.

I give all glory and honour to the Most High God!

In the eyes of the Creator,
every child counts.
Every child is a gift from God,
born with purpose and destiny.

Acknowledgements

I thank all of my Indigenous brothers and sisters for pouring out your hearts and sharing your stories so that your voices could be heard!

Thank you, John and Marion Franklin of *Imago*! This book has been an *Imago* project (www.imago-arts.org) and made possible through the generous support of donors. Thank you, precious donors!

Thank you Diane Roblyn Lee for walking through this 3 year book journey with me!

Many thanks to Daniel Holmes Photography for the portrait photo.

A special thank you to Henry and Jeanie Dunbar. It has been such a privilege to serve alongside you in the villages. I value your wisdom. The history you carry and shared with us regarding the reservations has been crucial in the development of chapter 11.

To my brother and sister, Fred and Alvina Thunderchild, you gave me a home, you have given me a family, you have made me feel so welcome; and for that I am eternally grateful!

Becky Thomas, you have been a special ministry partner and sister to create harmony with!

A big heartfelt thank you to Larry Willard, managing chief editor Marina Willard, and Castle Quay Books. I am so grateful for your wisdom, support, and oversight of this labour of love on every step of the journey.

Contents

Foreword

By Chief Kenny Blacksmith

Our people have a saying that when a child is born, "they came running in from a tree stump." So it was, on March 11, 1956, that I came running into the world of my Cree family. I was born in a tent in a place we called *paasikishcheukaau*, meaning "breakthrough to the other side". It refers to a portage that breaks through from one end to other.

Once, at the age of five, I was lying on the green grass in front of our tent, playing an imaginary game of hunting and walking through the grass that represented a great forest of trees. At one point, I looked around my surroundings and wondered,

"Who made the grass?"
I answered: "*Chishemandu*, the Great Spirit, did."

I looked at the water beyond and asked, "Who made the water?"
I answered: "*Chishemandu*, the Great Spirit, did."

I looked at the trees. "Who made the trees?"
I answered: "*Chishemandu*, the Great Spirit, did."

I looked at the sky above me. "Who made the sky?"
I answered: "*Chishemandu*, the Great Spirit, did."

I looked beyond the sky. "Who made the sun, the moon, and the stars?"

I answered: "*Chishemandu*, the Great Spirit, did."

Suddenly fear gripped me as I understood who *Chishemandu*, the Great Spirit, was! I ran into our tent and hung on to my mother's leg. Startled she turned to me and said, "My son, what is it?"

I looked up into her eyes and said, "Mom, I know who *Chishemandu*, the Great Spirit, is!"

This was the beginning of a prophetic life's journey of hearing, seeing, and encountering the heart of *Chishemandu*, the Great Spirit, who I now know as God.

I also know God is more than a Creator. He is my heavenly Father. He loves me, He has a plan and purpose for me, He is not going to harm me, and He will always be my hope and my future. He will lead to paths of prosperity in my mind, my emotions, my spirit, and my physical and natural well-being. He had a redemptive plan for me even before I was born in the bush. His Son Jesus became my personal Saviour, and the Holy Spirit, my comforter, my guide, and my help in times of need. God is now my refuge and my stronghold in times of uncertainty.

Here is a little bit of my story—which is like one of so many unique and distinct life stories across our nation captured by Belma Vardy, in her book, *Because The Spirit Was There*. The stories of these individuals deliver hope, healing, and freedom to our First Nations people across our country. She has captured stories and experiences into the windows of our First Nations communities and people who give life and meaning to the true identity of who we are in God.

Martin Luther King Jr. once said, "We must accept finite disappointment, but never lose infinite hope." I know now, "Those who hope in the LORD will renew their strength. They will soar on wings like eagles; they will run and not grow weary, they will walk and not be faint" (Isaiah 40:31).

Life can be difficult, and we can easily be held prisoners of an historic, deeply rooted negative past, but there is always breakthrough to the other side.

I also know we can hold unswervingly to the hope that God is faithful regarding His promises to us. He truly is the only covenant-making and covenant-keeping God we can trust. It's time to return to love, and to trust Him again. Forgiveness is key to opening the door to our healing and freedom from a negative past.

I know this:

He was always there from the very beginning of our life's journey.

He speaks Cree,

He's in the bush too!

—CHIEF KENNY BLACKSMITH
Cree Member of the Cree Nation of Mistissini, Quebec, Canada

Preface

Empty Cupboards, Full Hearts

By Belma Vardy

One morning I woke up wondering if I had really heard a voice say, "Buy Elizabeth some milk!"

I thought it odd. Why would I need to buy her milk? It didn't make sense to me. Both Elizabeth and her husband had good, professional jobs and certainly didn't, to my knowledge, need any help.

All throughout that day, the same thought kept running through my mind, over and over again. I call it a Holy Ghost nudge.

Finally, in the afternoon, I stopped resisting the thought and went to the store to buy three bags of milk. It seemed so silly. I was even embarrassed at the thought of calling Elizabeth. It made no sense.

At 10 p.m. that night, I knew I had to call. When Elizabeth answered, I said, "The Lord told me today to buy you some milk. You need to come and pick it up!"

"I'm in my pyjamas, but I'll come right over," she said.

Then I heard the voice again. This time, it said, "Clean out your cupboards and give all your food to Elizabeth."

"But I won't have any food left for myself," I replied. All was quiet, so I emptied my cupboards and packed up three bags of food.

Fifteen minutes later, Elizabeth was at my door. Sheepishly, I pointed to the bags on the counter and said, "There's the milk the Lord told me to buy for you. All those bags of food are for you too."

Elizabeth fell into my arms sobbing. "You don't know this, but four months ago my husband lost his job. This morning I woke up and cried out to the Lord, 'Jesus, I don't have any money to buy milk for my babies.' Now you're telling me you bought me some milk."

She wept in my arms. "The Lord heard my cry … and all this food! We have no money for food. This is such an answer to prayer." She went home, and I went to bed.

The next morning, at 7 a.m., I was getting ready to leave the house. As I opened my door, I gasped! I had almost tripped over three huge boxes. The first was filled with fresh meat, the second with fresh fruits and vegetables, and the third with canned goods, breads, and cereals.

I stood there in shock trying to take it all in. No one knew what had transpired between Elizabeth and me the night before—only God. My mind was spinning. Did an angel put this food here?

I was in a hurry to leave, but I pulled the boxes inside and dealt with the things that needed to go into the fridge. To my surprise, I heard a voice say, "Belma, unless you empty your cupboards, I cannot fill them."

Empty cupboards; empty pages. And that's how this book started—with empty pages. One by one, God brought the people who started filling them, giving windows into the First Nations culture and communities.

Little did I realize, when I began, the significance of those empty pages. Just as I was unaware of the depth of Elizabeth's need and the ministry God wanted to do in her life, Canada has been unaware of its need to hear the voice of our precious

Indigenous people who have been crying out in agony from the heart of our country.

I was already halfway through the writing of this book before the mass graves containing the remains of 215 innocent children were discovered at a residential school in Kamloops, B.C. It was then that God's purpose began to come more clearly into focus.

Most people are aware of the boarding schools Canada established to remove Indigenous children from their families and forcibly assimilate them into Canadian ways, but few understand the fallout in individual lives and families. Thousands of children were never returned to their homes, and no explanations were offered or available. The children simply disappeared. They became the "missing children".

I begin the journey of this book on the downtown Eastside Vancouver streets, where the shadows of direct and indirect experiences in residential schools have touched almost every life, but these stories are not just about history; they're about the ability of God to transform lives.

Much of the hopelessness evident on so many faces is a reflection of the lack of understanding and the absence of being believed. Until now the voice of the Indigenous people has not been sought, heard, or valued.

The stories that follow are not told for the purpose of gaining pity; they're about sharing hearts longing to be heard, acknowledged, honoured, believed, and understood.

Only God's outstretched arms offer true restoration of what has been stolen. He offers genuine healing.

Chapter 1

A Bit of History

In 1993, I, Belma, was given the opportunity to serve in a ministry of compassion with Indigenous people. Their chiefs invited me to share my story and participate in their communities. During that time, I developed a deep love for our Native people and a profound desire to see them experience cultural redemption. Through our interactions we uncovered surprising common ground.

First, I too had suffered under a misguided regime ruling Germany during my early childhood, and later under the oppression of an extremely abusive parent. During this time, I was in forced separation from my loving and nurturing father. I immediately understood the parallel with the Native children's experiences of being sent to abusive residential schools far from their loved ones. We were drawn together in a kinship and common bond.

A deep sadness and grief that breeds hopelessness fills the air of tribal communities. According to the chiefs, my story dispels grief because I found the way to cross the divide from hopelessness to healing. When I tell my story, Indigenous people identify with it. The chiefs encourage me to share in hope that their people will receive healing and freedom through it.

During the years that I have travelled to Indigenous communities and taught in the mean streets of Vancouver's Eastside, stories of the same hope and redemption I found have emerged in community after community. Now I am no longer sharing just my story, as I did in my first book, *Because God*

Was There, but also the stories of others who live in the light of hope.

If you feel like you are on the outside looking in because you don't know, or maybe don't understand, Canadian history, I'll share a brief overview in this introductory chapter. But if you are already familiar with it, you may want to go on to the chapters where you will find the personal stories of hope and healing among the First Nations people.

A Tragic History

The term "residential schools" is synonymous with "boarding schools" in most cultures, but for Native people, the thought of residential schools stirs memories of agony, angst, and horror.

Residential schools were the misguided plan of the government that became the root of the trauma inflicted upon the precious Indigenous peoples of Canada. The motive was the intentional destruction of the family and the removal of their language as a means of forcing assimilation. How did it all begin?

The Canadian government viewed the Indigenous people almost as a subspecies without value. As a result, we have been told that by the late 1800s they had what they called "an Indian problem". The Aboriginal people of North America had been "conquered" and almost obliterated, but because they determinedly maintained their culture and uniqueness, the government decided they really hadn't been defeated. Their position was "Kill the Indian, save the man," with the assumption that removal of culture, values, beliefs, and heritage from young children in their developmental years would assimilate them into white culture.

To solve the so-called problem, the plan was to forcibly remove the children from their parents and indoctrinate them into white culture.

Government representatives thundered into Native communities claiming that the parents' homes were unfit for the raising of children or that the parents were unqualified. They kidnapped children ages three to five and took them to distant facilities, the closest being an hour-and-a-half drive or what was a two-and-a-half-day journey a hundred years ago. We can only imagine the terror both these abducted young children and their parents experienced at the separation.

From the moment the children were delivered to the schools, everything changed. Workers immediately cut boys' hair into brush cuts and chopped off the girls' long, shiny black hair into short bowl cuts. The staff took their clothes—including ribbon shirts—and burned them, replacing them with white-child dresses, button-down shirts, and pants. Instead of skin-soft moccasins and bear-hide boots, they were outfitted in saddle shoes with laces.

Food, schedules, priorities, and language changed as well. These bewildered and frightened little ones were not even allowed to communicate in their Native tongue. It was considered a breach of protocol for a child to ask questions. If they ventured a simple "Where am I?", they would risk being slapped.

In some schools, visitors including moms and dads were not allowed. At the same time, children were rarely allowed to leave the schools. Some were permitted to go home occasionally, while others were not.

The mistreatment and control at many of the schools was often inhumane. Yet not all schools were equally oppressive. The staff at some genuinely wanted to help the children. At others, they carried out their mandate to isolate them in an indescribably tragic manner, causing the residential school experience for many to be compared to living in the harsh conditions of a concentration camp.

Darkness was pervasive.

Fear filled the air.

Survival was a daily struggle.

Punishment was constant.

Abuse was rampant at every level—physical, emotional, and sexual.

The entire initiative resulted in unimaginably difficult times for the little ones and their families. It is remembered as an ugly blot on Canadian history. Records show that about half the children died—thousands of them. When a child died, they simply disappeared with no memorial service, no notification to the parents and no record of death.

Most disturbing, while the program was initiated and funded by the government, the church implemented and ran it. Priests, pastors, and missionaries were the authorities and teachers. Consequently, words like *church*, *God*, *Bible*, and *religion* became synonymous with kidnap, abuse, death, and separation in the memory banks of Native people.

Today, mental health professionals say that the trauma these generations have endured was much like post-traumatic stress disorder (PTSD). It has filtered down through the generations as a nasty curse.

Yet, despite the inordinate pressure and loss, Indigenous people were not assimilated, even though much of their cultural identity disappeared, and what was retained became distorted. They lost their cultural knowledge of survival skills and the desire to hunt and trap food. The communal nature of their culture was broken, and precious bonds among family and community were lost. With a lack of love at the schools, the children had learned how to be alone, disconnected, and abused.

The trauma of what happened to the Native culture and community is a fact. It happened. It's history. Hardly any Indigenous soul has been untouched, either directly or indirectly, by the pain inflicted on individuals and families through the boarding school era of cultural genocide that began in 1890 and continued throughout the twentieth century, with the last school closing in 1996.

One of my favourite related Scriptures for us as believers to express toward the Indigenous people is Colossians 3:12 and 14: "As God's chosen people, holy and dearly loved, clothe yourselves with compassion, kindness, humility, gentleness and patience ... And over all these virtues put on love, which binds them all together in perfect unity." Here Paul is talking to the Colossians, but also to us—God's chosen people, holy and dearly loved. It's amazing to think that the Creator of the universe knows each of our names and says we are dearly loved. Our responsibility is to live our lives with the compassion, kindness, and love with which He loved us.

Recovery

In Native culture, healing is a powerful word. It is used all the time within the context of the individual being helped in all four components—physical, mental, spiritual, and emotional. It addresses healing of relationships and of community. With the "Idle No More" movement, the core issue is healing our land, referencing natural resources and the water that's being polluted.

What all Indigenous villages and tribes have in common is the loss of their culture and identity. This is more significant and devastating to them than the loss of their land.

The only true hope for the way ahead for all of us comes through removing the *power of the trauma* through the *power and love of the Holy Spirit*.

At this time in history much has been exposed. Truth is emerging and restoration has begun.

I invite you now to come with Becky Thomas and me as we visit the First Nations Bible College in downtown Eastside, Vancouver and meet some amazing people.

Chapter 2

The Mean Streets:
Door Between Realities

Not raining, but no sun; a netherworld between realities. I, Belma, opened the passenger door to get out, but the Eastside Vancouver sidewalk was ugly. The stench of old urine mixed with weed and hopelessness assaulted my nostrils. My mind made the connection: this sidewalk resembled the ones facing the glitzy boutiques and bistros of nearby Gastown, with its grey hardness of the concrete, but there all resemblance ended.

Someone had obviously tried to clear the area in front of the First Nations Bible College, where we were headed, but no one had yet been able to fix the lives of the bodies hunched and hurting against brick walls as far down the street as the eye could see. While the empty syringes had been swept into the trash, their contents remained in the ravaged bodies of those who made the street their home. This could have been Mumbai, or today's Los Angeles—but Vancouver, one of the world's most desirable cities?

A young man in his early twenties—someone's son—was slumped against a wall sleeping, backpack strapped to his skinny body. I placed my right foot on the sidewalk, breathed in the fog, and glanced to my right, antennas up in this foreign world. A man with no front teeth was rocking back and forth, yelling obscenities at the top of his lungs. Four guys on my left, alone together, were shooting up. Two men beside a church sign lay shaking on the waste-stained concrete. I shivered. A couple of women leaning against the wall sought comfort in a hit. A drunk, pushing a shopping cart and singing a song, staggered by, almost stumbling into the car door. In the shopping cart was a grown man curled up, crying like a baby.

My friend Becky Thomas and I had responded to an invitation from Pastor Randy Barnetson (director of the only First Nations Bible college in Canada) to teach here, in one of Canada's most needy areas. Becky is of mixed blood, her Native heritage being Cherokee. She wrote the study guide for my first book.

Randy and Cheryl Bear Barnetson had started the Bible college in the mid-'90s to train people to serve in Indigenous communities. Cheryl Bear's First Nations community is Nadleh Whut'en First Nation in British Columbia, Canada. She is from Dumdenyoo Clan (Bear Clan). Their hearts burned to equip First Nations people to become pastors, evangelists, church planters, missionaries, and leaders to their own people, using First Nations' expressions and cultural context.

Besides his busy role in the Bible college, Randy continued to pastor Street Church until his untimely death in 2020. The church and the college shared a common space, equipped with a kitchen. Many of the Indigenous members and students were former street folk saved under Randy's ministry. He and Cheryl discipled them in God's Word through the Bible college and poured into them sacrificially, right from the beginning. These people, in turn, went on with their lives to make other disciples. You will read some of their testimonies here.

That day, I looked up at the church sign. It read simply "Street Church" and featured a stark black-and-white drawing of the head of Jesus. Right around the corner from the free-needle clinic, the church served the nation's poorest, in one of the most destitute communities in North America. To this day, users continue to frequent the free-needle clinic to take their drugs under the savvy eyes of Overdose Prevention Society staff, who hand out clean syringes and stand ready to intervene with oxygen and the emergency drug naloxone. The place opens at eight in the morning and is full by ten. It stays busy until closing at nine. More than two thousand homeless and addicted people live in this area on the streets, doing what they can to care for each other.

This is ground zero for Canada's opioid crisis—a killing ground where the weapon of mass destruction is a needle that shoots poison into bloodstreams. Breathing slows to a halt in junk-filled alleyways, toilet stalls, and lonely stairwells. Over half of the paramedic responses to suspected-overdose calls come from downtown Eastside.

I closed the car door and paused, shocked and in sorrow. I lowered my head. I had been told this place was the last stop before the coffin. By the time people get here, they are on their way to the grave.

Becky grabbed my arm and said, "We need to get off this street." She pulled me along toward the sign. We made the long climb up the narrow, steep staircase into the Bible college, where Pastor Randy and twelve students greeted us with joy. They were all First Nations students, except for one African.

Five hours later, following insightful introductions to students and staff, a morning class and an annual meeting, it was time to leave. The door between sanity and insanity reopened. There, beside the door, stood the same young man, still slumped against the wall sleeping, backpack still strapped to his skinny body, the half-eaten box of Voortman cookies still lying on the sidewalk beside him.

Here at 175 East Hastings Street in the heart of downtown Vancouver, B.C., stories of human degradation unfold every day.

Perhaps because of the early desperation of my own life, I feel a tremendous bond with these precious Indigenous brothers and sisters whose lives are changed through the love of God. These are some of their stories.

Saved Twice
Allan Williams's Story

To fully understand the story of Allan Williams and the depth of the miracle God has performed, one needs to walk in his scuffed moccasins as he grew up on Vancouver Island's oldest northern community, the small northern town of Alert Bay, B.C.

Alert Bay sits nestled near Port McNeill on Cormorant Island, in traditional Kwakwaka'wakw First Nations territory. It was named in the late 1860s for the Royal Navy ship HMS *Alert*, which conducted survey operations in the area. With a population of close to 1,500, half of whom are First Nations people, the town is a blend of aboriginal and pioneer culture. It boasts the world's tallest totem pole.

Once a thriving fishing village, the shores of the tiny (1.8 square kilometer) island tell the story of days gone by when the fish-salting plant and Navy survey operations were the central activities around which people lived out their lives. The abundant wildlife is still evident. Seabirds, humpback whales, orca, grey whales, sea lions, and white-sided dolphins all flourish in the surrounding waters.

One can imagine young Allan Williams skipping stones in the grey waters and squinting his black eyes to watch shiny-backed whales sound off the coast.

Today's waterfront boardwalks, marinas, and ferries may have replaced the early culture, but memories of government initiatives to bleach away the rich potlatch customs of dance and song have not been forgotten. No efforts to import the trendiness of Vancouver Island tea shops to the streets of Alert Bay can mask the horror of the history of families torn apart in this community when precious young ones were relocated to residential schools. Confusion replaced time-honoured traditions. All that was familiar in the culture of the tiny island was torn from the lives of both those taken and those left behind.

As though taking the children was not enough, in 1921, under Section 116 of the Indian Act, government officials confiscated all the wooden masks, copper shields, and dance regalia they could find in the area. Following long and tedious negotiations in the 1970s and '80s, the artifacts were eventually returned and housed in a museum, the U'mista Cultural Centre, but the trauma left deep scars of loss and outrage.

Allan says, "I am the youngest out of seven kids. My brother and sisters went to Residential School. I am the lucky one in my family. I never went to res school. Although I didn't go, I still had a rough life growing up on the reserve, getting verbally, physically, and emotionally abused. It was so painful it's hard to talk about it.

"I moved off the reserve between 1979 and 1980. From there, I wandered up and down Vancouver Island from Port Hardy to Nanaimo until 1983. In 1984, I moved here to Vancouver and I have been here ever since. Although I was off and on living a Christian life over the past fifteen years, now I am finally following my heart and my calling to becoming a pastor. It's been a rough couple of years, but now I am fighting and facing my past and going forward with my life. Randy Barnetson and the First Nations Bible College has helped me with that. I know the Lord will lead me in the right direction. How I love my Lord and Jesus now with all my heart."

Allan says: "I feel so thankful—I was saved from going to Residential School and saved from that life of pain."

Allan's words simply testify of the ability of God to go to the bottom of a deeply wounded heart and restore it to fullness of purpose.

Chapter 3

Stories Within the Great Story

First Nations Bible College
(Ministry Trip One, October 2018)[1]

Fifteen new students this year!

Their faces were eager and full of hope; bright, black eyes so hungry to learn—so contrary to the faces on the street. It was exhilarating to know that God has a special plan for each one, but I could see the pain—the scars from their worlds: addictions, sex trafficking, prostitution, stripping, deformities, and abuses of every kind. They were so desperate to learn the Word of God that they sometimes stayed in shelters, because housing was limited.

Here the students were taught to lead worship, preach, and serve the poor. Tuition was free and people could start anytime. Everyone was accepted and welcomed. Intensives were one week long, and new ones began each Tuesday. One hundred courses in theology and practical ministry skills were taught in three-year cycles. Students needed to accumulate at least forty courses to graduate. The two-year program led to a diploma and ministerial credentials.

Many didn't have money for books and food, so Randy Barnetson provided funds from the church budget and from his own pocket, while adding one hot meal daily for each student.

---

1. A very special thank you to Daniel Holmes, who drove us endless hours, chauffeuring us back and forth from our home-away-from-home to the First Nations Bible College and Street Church every day as we ministered. Special thanks to Marilyn Wishart, who accompanied us on this trip to pray.

Randy tried to find ways to help look after the students until they got on their feet with jobs and tools for independent living. He took them on outreaches at least twice a year. They didn't travel in luxury, but they experienced what it was like to serve in local ministries on First Nation Reservations and in the inner cities of the USA and Canada.

First-year students were all trained to preach at Street Church. Drug addicts and street people knew that if they showed up three nights a week at church, they'd get two hot dogs and hear worship music and the gospel message. When they heard how Jesus had changed the lives of people just like them, they received tremendous hope for their own lives.

Within ten minutes of arriving, Becky and I started teaching. Our theme was "Finding *your* story within the *great* story."

We told the students they'd each have three minutes to share their stories at the end of the week at Street Church. The idea was to help them organize their thoughts and give them the confidence to begin sharing their testimonies.

When Friday came, Becky and I reminded the students that they would have the opportunity to share three-minute versions of their stories at Street Church that night.

With the average attendance being 150 to 200 people each night, we watched as many of the street people helped drag each other up the steep staircase, just to have a chair to sit on and get their two free hot dogs.

The first student of the night got up to share a bit of his story and then boomed, "You must be born again!" He shared some Scripture and ended with a salvation prayer. I said to Becky, "What happened to the story? This is preaching!" It was amazing!

The second student to share was Lloyd. Two years earlier he had been homeless, on drugs, feeling hopeless and alone along with the other drug addicts on the street. He told how he had sat on the sidewalk crying out, "I want a father! I wish I had a father!" A passerby said to him, "I will take you to meet the Father, but before you meet your Father, you need to be introduced to His Son."

He got up and accompanied the person to Street Church. The next day, when he awoke, he realized he had no desire for drugs. He said, "I know my Father's love because Jesus died on the cross for my sins."

One by one, the students, all of whom had lived on the streets, preached stormy sermons as the homeless visitors ate their hot dogs. All had a passion to see the street people come into a relationship with their Saviour.

Our first visit together to the Bible college had a profound impact on both Becky and me. It stirred in me a passion to return.

I Want a Father
Lloyd Major's Story

Lloyd Major lived on the street for twelve years. In all those years, he never had shelter or regular meals. His food came from garbage picking, but he had a heart of compassion that extended far beyond his own needs. He fed rats every night. Starting out with four, he ended up with fifty. Petty cash came from collecting pop bottles.

Lloyd lived like the other drug addicts on the street; homeless, on drugs, feeling hopeless and alone. He never dreamt of anything beyond life on the street. But then—God showed up. Here's what happened, in Lloyd's own words:

"One day I ran out of dope. I realized I was all alone. I cried for the first time in twelve years. I needed help. I didn't know who I was crying out to.

"I was sitting on the sidewalk crying, 'I want a father. I wish I had a father.' Someone walking by said to me, 'I will take you to meet the Father; but before you meet your Father, you need to be introduced to His Son.' He sat down and spent time talking to me.

"When I woke up the next day, I had no desire for drugs. I know my Father's love, because Jesus died on the cross for me.

"The person who introduced me to my Father took me by the hand and walked alongside me on the road to recovery. I graduated from my third year of First Nations Bible College after earning my way through by working nights cleaning. The Lord gave me custodial work for three years. Now I volunteer at Potter's Place Mission on Hastings Street in Vancouver. Many Saturday nights, I preached at Street Church, under the mentorship of Randy Barnetson, filling in for Pastor Mike. I pray for all the street people and keep sharing the love of Jesus with everyone possible on the street."

Note: Lloyd is now ordained and works as an assistant pastor in downtown Eastside. He also continues to preach at the Living Waters Church and Potter's Place Mission on Hastings, praying with many people and spreading the love of Jesus wherever he goes, letting people know, "God is my everything."

Ladies' Nite, Lindy's Light
First Nations Bible College
(Ministry Trip Two, October 2019)

Tuesday was my first full day of teaching at First Nations Bible College. I threw my leather bag, filled with the needs of the day, over my shoulder and double-wrapped my scarf for the commute. It was a windy day, about to be filled with God incidents.

God had opened this door, and I was ready for unknown challenges ahead. I learned a long time ago that ministry is not about me. As long as I kept my focus on God, He would use me to do whatever He wanted in the lives of the people here.

After the first class, Jenn Allan, a First Nations Bible College graduate and, at the time, pastor in training, asked me if I would help her write out her testimony. As she began sharing details of her life, pain surfaced and tears began to flow. Words stumbled across her lips, as she tried to find adequate ways of expressing the horror of fourteen years of surviving in the sex trade and enduring family members ripped from their homes and relocated to residential schools.

Despite the raw emotion, we pushed through it all, and, three hours later it was on paper after ten minutes of giving God the glory for rescuing her. She ended with this Scripture: "'I know the plans I have for you,' declares the LORD, 'plans to prosper you and not to harm you, plans to give you hope and a future'" (Jeremiah 29:11). Her full testimony can be found in the section "Out from The Sex Trade—Forever Free: Jenn Allan's Story" in chapter 3.

Jenn's story was truly amazing—a recounting of events, ending with an encouragement to people to give God all the glory. Besides starting a support group outreach called Jenn's Kitchen, she ran a weekly group called Ladies' Nite from six to nine p.m.

Jenn knew all the prostitutes in Vancouver East Side. She continued to walk the streets, but only to invite the women and girls personally to Ladies' Nite. No men allowed! It had to be a safe place for the women.

Every Tuesday night, Jenn put a sign in front of the church doors that read "Ladies' Nite—Come for Food and Drinks" and propped up a menu.

This was Tuesday—my first full day. The women were about to arrive for Ladies' Nite at Street Church! I was excited to help buy food and set up. I helped Jenn get the tables ready. We fussed as much as the budget would allow and made do with the rest. We decorated the counter with flowers and arranged the snacks and food, but according to Jenn, there weren't enough varieties of snacks. She invited me to go with her to buy some more.

I nervously stuck close to her as we made our way through the maze of blank stares on the sidewalk. Tales of grey zombies haunted my thoughts as we passed men and women lost in drug and alcohol stupors. Every few yards, I heard a cheerful greeting from Jenn—"Hi, Joan, tonight is the Ladies' Nite! Come for a hot meal at six o'clock!" Woman after woman received the invitation.

At the store, Jenn carefully chose snacks. "We can't have this one because it is too hard on their teeth. This makes them too thirsty later. This isn't healthy enough. I want them to have something nutritious." So much love and care!

Jenn welcomed the walk back through the maze of drug addicts and prostitutes and used it as an opportunity to invite more women.

I was relieved to get back safely to our familiar environment.

It was a feast that night: hot dogs and hot coffee on the menu again, but that didn't matter; warm foods for empty bellies, served with love. Jenn also made some spaghetti and a salad. That week, a bakery in Gastown had donated some pastries—a special treat.

When the women arrived out of the cold at six, they were welcomed into a warm, safe refuge with low lighting and soft worship music—a cozy, comfortable environment with a buffet of hot meals with salads and desserts to awaken their appetites. It was a disarming environment where hardened souls could relax and experience the love of Jesus.

We had barely opened the doors when the ladies began to show up. Some were regulars who obviously knew the territory, but others were new and unsure of what to do. Everyone received a personal welcome while some needed introductions to feel part of the group. They sat and talked while eating, recounting incidents of survival, escape, and struggle. Afterward, they visited racks of clothes, selecting and taking according to their choosing.

Most important, they were given the gift of caring time and, if they asked for it, prayer.

I stayed in the background in a dimly lit area, observing and praying silently, available to Jenn if she needed help. To my surprise, one of the women came to me and asked if I could pray for her.

Lindy looked weathered and was emotionally distraught. She was probably in her forties, but the drugs had etched deep lines more often seen in faces of those in their sixties or older. She reached out a shaky hand tentatively to me, then grabbed me by the arm and looked me right in the eye—her eyes full of fear. With a voice of desperation, she choked out the words: "I need prayer. I get forced to take these drugs. I don't want to take them anymore. Please pray that I don't have to take them anymore. Please help me." She hung her head. In shame, she grabbed my hands and held them tight.

I had no idea what to do or say, but I heard myself telling her how much God loves her. I wanted her to know she wasn't alone. I started telling her how God was with her all the time, but then I felt something on my pant legs; her tears were flowing and splashing on both legs of my jeans. It was like a small tap had been opened. As she sobbed out her pain, I sang to her, "Oh, how He loves you and me. Oh, how He loves you and me. He bled and died, what more could He give? Oh, how He loves you. Oh, how He loves me. Oh, how He loves you and me."

Gradually, gradually, her tears abated and she regained some composure. I knew she needed to meet Jesus as her friend and Saviour, and so I asked her if she'd like to open her heart and let Him be part of her life. She said yes, nodded her head, and repeated the sinner's prayer with me.

Lindy had hung her head throughout the entire prayer, and as I finished, she raised it and looked at me. I was shocked to see a dramatic change in her countenance. She looked completely different! Her face was beaming! She had the biggest smile and even her eyes were smiling! Twinkling! She was full of joy.

I then noticed a breathtaking brilliance radiating around her, and another big light encircling her. I was in awe. Lindy just kept smiling at me as her grip on my hands became tighter. She'd been holding them tight the whole time. I started singing, "Amen, Hallelujah, Amen, Hallelujah, Amen, Amen, Amen." To my surprise, she started singing along with me. Over and over again, we sang that chorus while our eyes locked with each other. We were in complete unity. As we sang, I heard more than just our two voices. It was surround sound. Who and where were the voices coming from? Were the angels singing with us?

Lindy's eyes wouldn't leave mine. She looked deep into my soul as we sang that chorus over and over again. It was like heaven had come down and swallowed us up in its purest, holiest atmosphere. We were oblivious to any people around us. It seemed like we were the only two in the room and we were immersed in the love of the Father. His thick presence enfolded us—a supernatural connection. Such a precious moment! And all the while no one else seemed to notice our encounter with God, and each other.

An amazing sense of unity flowed during the evening as Jenn related to the women at Ladies' Nite.

They knew she was one of them, and yet she was different. She had what they all wanted and she made it clear that God's love was there and available for each and every one of them. It was the love of Jesus, who wanted to be their friend, counsellor, helper, and advocate with their heavenly Father.

And then there was Lindy, whose glowing smile never left. She remained enveloped in the bright light, her eyes sparkling with life as we sat together for what seemed like a very long time in the presence of God's glory. It was such a special night.

Out From the Sex Trade — Forever Free
Jenn Allan's Story

Jenn Allan was born in Whitehorse, Yukon, and comes from Tlingit Nations. The Tlingit tribe has ties to Haida and Tsimshian tribes of Canada. They were trading partners for centuries. Tlingit blankets, baskets, and jewelry were known for extraordinary craftsmanship, while Haidas supplied sturdy cedar dugout canoes that Tlingits used for fishing, hunting, and trading and for warfare. Their lands provided an abundant supply of food, and their waters teemed with fish, otters, and seals. The forests were rich with berries to gather and deer and bears to hunt. Traditionally, Tlingit women cared for children, gathered plants to feed the family, and cooked. The men hunted, fished, and protected the tribe. Life was structured, sustainable, and reasonably predictable, until the coming of the white man changed everything.

The lush forests of the Yukon are a long way from the mean streets of downtown Eastside, Vancouver.

One day, long before Jenn was born, when her mother Irma Scarff was just a four-year-old child playing with her corn-husk doll, the government people arrived unannounced, tore the little ones from the arms of their screaming parents, and loaded the children into trucks. After a terrifying, bumpy drive that separated them from all that was familiar, they were thrust into the dormitories of residential schools, where the loving arms of their parents were replaced by physical and sexual abuse perpetrated by steely-eyed strangers. That's where Irma Scarff endured her formative years.

When Irma was twelve, she hitchhiked to Vancouver and was swept up into the world of heroin addiction. Within a year, she was supporting her $120-a-day habit by stealing everything that wasn't nailed down. Soon, she became an enforcer, keeping slave-traded girls in line for their pimps. Having turned off her feelings, she had no problem hurting the girls to make sure they didn't escape.

When Irma was eighteen years old, she got pregnant but didn't know it. When she realized it, she tapered down the amount of heroin she was using but kept partying. She had slept with so many different men that she had no clue which one was the father.

One night, as she was leaving a house party, she slipped on the cold November ice and fell flat on her stomach—very alarming for a pregnant woman, who could lose her child from such an accident. She was rushed to the hospital and gave birth to a two-months-premature, three-pound, eight-ounce baby girl. The child was addicted to heroin. The doctors told Irma that the baby was too small and would die within seventy-two hours, because her body wasn't fully developed.

Irma sat in the hallway, her hands covering her ears to block the soul-wracking screams of her little girl who needed a fix. Irma's mother had the priest baptize the child, and both women left the hospital expecting the baby to die. Irma went back to the bars to party.

But the little scrap of humanity—Jenn Allan—survived.

Months after the two women left the hospital, the nurse called Jenn's grandmother and asked, "Is anyone coming to pick up this baby girl?" and added, "If not, we're calling Social Services." Both grandparents were shocked she was still alive. They collected little Jenn from the hospital and raised her for the next three and a half years. Their daughter, Irma, was tracked down and told to go back to the Yukon to raise her child. But Irma kept drinking and using. Only occasionally was Jenn in her mother's care. She was raised mainly by her grandparents.

One night when little Jenn was three and a half, Irma was high on drugs and in a drunken rage. She got into a fight with her sister over a boyfriend and stabbed her to death. She was sentenced to twelve years for manslaughter and was sent to the prison for women in Kingston, Ontario. According to Irma, heroin was more available in prison than it was on the street.

Sadly, Jenn's grandmother got sick and asked her aunt to raise Jenn in Nova Scotia. Jenn's aunt had also been raised in a residential school and consequently had no understanding of how to raise children. She became physically abusive toward the little girl for the next four years. When the situation became untenable, Jenn was placed in the foster care system.

Any hopes of finding a safe place to land were dashed for Jenn when, in the first foster home, she was sexually abused. The owners of the second home were at a loss to know what to do with her, and the third placement simply supplied food and a bed until Social Services found a permanent placement for the child.

Thankfully, the fourth foster home was better. It was run by a Christian lady and her husband. Jenn lived there for nine years and aged out of the foster care system in her late teens.

Having reconnected with her birth family at age seventeen, Jenn was hopeful, thinking it might be for the better that Family and Social Services felt it was good to send her back to live with them. The government bought her a plane ticket to Prince Rupert, B.C., and she left with great dreams of starting life afresh with her own people.

Out of prison by then, Jenn's mother, Irma, was totally incapable of looking after herself and was so filled with anger that she was a danger to herself and anyone who dared cross her path. She had finally made it home to Whitehorse but had nothing in her to give to her daughter. When she discovered that she was pregnant again, Irma determined to get clean, because she couldn't bear to think of this baby having to go through the horrendous withdrawal that her first baby, Jenn, had experienced. When she discovered that her old drug buddy was now a born-again Christian minister, she responded to his suggestion that she should discover the cure that worked for him and went to his church. As soon as she entered the building, she knew she wanted "what those people had", and there was no turning back. She gave her life to Jesus and, today, goes wherever she's called to help people become free of addictions.

That amazing transformation had not yet begun, however, when Jenn first returned to Whitehorse. Irma was still an addict at that point. Jenn and her cousins started to party together. One night, they went into a bar and met a thirty-year-old fellow who invited them to his house party. Jenn got separated from her cousins, who left her there with strangers. These people introduced her to the sex and drug trade, and she was forced to learn as she went along. In the beginning, she made $400 per date and had to give half to her pimp. In no time, her pimp was taking all the money and she was forced to do dates without any payment.

Life in the sex trade wore Jenn down on every level—emotionally, spiritually, and physically. Drugs became her sad solace. By the time she was twenty-four years old, she was addicted to crack and alcohol. Sex slavery was her life. She was working the strolls in Vancouver's downtown Eastside, having lost all hope for a future. She was angry at society and saw no way out to change her life. It was at that point that she bumped into a Christian organization—the Salvation Army.

Jenn had grown to love Jesus along the way, but she associated the Bible with her mother's residential school experience and the foster system and hated His followers. She had never experienced real Christian love but instead felt constantly judged. Too many so-called Christians had criticized her and told her what a bad woman she was. To her, Christianity was all about rules and regulations, but the Salvation Army Unit 614 was different. They treated her like a person, called her by name, and invited her to Bible studies. She developed a warm, genuine community of friends. By the time she was twenty-six years old, she had quit crack. Six months later, she was mercifully able to get out of the sex trade. From the streets, she was helped into Christian recovery housing and started to trust Jesus to help rebuild her life. She went to addiction and trauma counselling twice a week and attended regular Bible studies.

In 2013, Jenn felt Jesus direct her to become a Salvation Army soldier. She went to the Salvation Army Bible college, War College, and two years later, graduated with a new uniform and an associated degree in practical ministry. From there, she went to Randy Barnetson's First Nations Bible College and finished a three-year program in seventeen months with a diploma in pastoral training. She then completed a year of seminary and graduated with a certificate in transformation leadership, completing a practicum at the Street Church as an assistant pastor.

Psalm 91:1–16 will always resonate deeply in Jenn's heart because of the way Jesus kept her safe and alive while she was in constant danger:

> Whoever dwells in the shelter of the Most High
>   will rest in the shadow of the Almighty.
> I will say of the LORD, "He is my refuge and my fortress,
>   my God, in whom I trust."
> Surely he will save you
>   from the fowler's snare
>   and from the deadly pestilence.
> He will cover you with his feathers,
>   and under his wings you will find refuge;
>   his faithfulness will be your shield and rampart.
> You will not fear the terror of night,
>   nor the arrow that flies by day,

nor the pestilence that stalks in the darkness,
    nor the plague that destroys at midday.
A thousand may fall at your side,
    ten thousand at your right hand,
    but it will not come near you.
You will only observe with your eyes
    and see the punishment of the wicked.
If you say, "The LORD is my refuge,"
    and you make the Most High your dwelling,
no harm will overtake you,
    no disaster will come near your tent.
For he will command his angels concerning you
    to guard you in all your ways;
they will lift you up in their hands,
    so that you will not strike your foot against a stone.
You will tread on the lion and the cobra;
    you will trample the great lion and the serpent.
"Because he loves me," says the LORD, "I will rescue him;
    I will protect him, for he acknowledges my name.
He will call on me, and I will answer him;
    I will be with him in trouble,
    I will deliver him and honor him.
With long life I will satisfy him
    and show him my salvation."

On Tuesday nights, from six to nine p.m., Jenn ran Ladies' Nite for the oppressed women of Vancouver's Eastside. With food, treats, and drinks, she poured God's abundant love out on the most marginalized of the city's street women, from rape victims to survival sex workers. Her purpose was to demonstrate the love of Jesus to them in a way that would look after their practical needs. She supplied food hampers, hot meals, clothes, goody bags, facials, and manicures. In this way, the women got a genuine taste of God's love and the love of the church for them.

Apart from her Ladies' Nite ministry, Jenn works as an over-dose prevention worker in downtown Eastside. Prior to Randy Barnetson's death, she also ran Midnight Ministries, where she took Bible college students out walking through the back allies. Wherever there was medical distress or the need to check on people, pray for anyone, or escort assault victims to the hospital, Jenn and the students were there to serve the needs of the street people.

In reference to Randy Barnetson, Jenn says, "I am so grateful to have been mentored by Pastor Randy. He was one of the kindest pastors I met in the downtown Eastside."

Jenn's life today is a reflection of her steadfast commitment to serve her Saviour and her people. Back in the day, when she was attending First Nations Bible College, she met worship leader John Riley at Street Church, while he too was a student at the college. Half Nova Scotian Mi'kmaq and half Irish, John won Jenn's heart. They worked together for two years at Street Church, then became engaged, and married January 4, 2021.

Initially, they were both living in nice places in the west end of the lower mainland of Vancouver, but both felt God's leading to move to the downtown Eastside to live among the people. Jenn says, "Jesus lived among the people. He taught. He didn't leave and go live in a nice mansion somewhere and come back. He stayed with the people He was teaching." They moved into a single-room occupancy in downtown Eastside, where they were available for street ministry, day or night.

After completing their Bible course on hermeneutics, "How to Interpret the Bible," at Global University, John and Jenn were ordained, and they now serve as assistant pastors to the assistant bishop of the First Pentecostal Evangel Church of Canada in Vancouver. Jenn is continuing her work with overdose prevention.

The couple continues to lead Midnight Ministries, doing outreach from midnight to 2:30 a.m. every night. Together, they walk the back alleys, talk to people, pray with them, hand out food, respond to medical emergencies (such as drug overdoses), and escort people to hospitals and shelters.

Lately, Jenn has held Ladies' Nite on the street with a Christian band. She preaches the gospel, provides life-giving Christian music, and gives manicures from midnight to two a.m. to brighten the lives of desperate women.

Jenn and her mother, Irma, connect on a regular basis. Irma is extremely proud of her daughter and new son-in-law—the first pastors in the family.

Jenn asks, "How many drug-addicted sex workers have become not only survivors but pastors?" She goes on to say, "When I tell my story, no one can say it's impossible for a sex worker to become a pastor. Everyone knows it's next to impossible to leave the sex trade. Most sex workers die in the sex trade … like the Picton Case. My story is a testimony to God's power and proves He exists!"

[On May 7, 2022, at 7:06 a.m., Irma Scarff was promoted to glory, to be with her beloved Jesus.]

Chapter 4

More Stories of Transformation

The following testimonies are stories of transformed lives, true stories of God's grace being poured out on some of the staff and students of the Street Church and First Nations Bible College. These are just a few examples of ordinary people who allowed the extraordinary love of God to change their lives.

Jailbreak! Out for Life
John Gordon Riley's Story

Half Mi'kmaq First Nation, half Irish, John Riley was born with a powerful Christian heritage. This is his story.

From the age of thirteen to twenty-three, John defined himself as a Satanist and was consciously committed to serving the dark lord. Forever tuned to his satanic music, watching satanic movies, and reading the satanic bible, his mantra was "Hail, Satan."

When John committed armed robbery, he was caught, tried, and sentenced to one year in prison.

While in jail, John was exposed to church and read some books that he had never before seen. One that particularly caught his attention was an ex-Hell's Angel's story about being transformed by the love and power of Jesus Christ.

While the dark lord had led him to jail, it was Jesus who led him out, three weeks short of completing his sentence.

Once back out on the street, John's mom, who was a believer in Christ, made a deal with her son. She said, "If you come to church with me for one year, I will bring you home." John agreed to the terms, and she paid for his fare home. He faithfully attended her church, Queensway Cathedral in Etobicoke, and that's where John met a new friend, Rob Glenn. They both accepted Christ, and John enrolled in Teen Challenge, Toronto, where his life was powerfully impacted by amazing teaching and discipling from godly mentors.

Tragically, Rob was murdered, but John went on to become involved in the wrestling industry for fifteen years, standing for Jesus—hardcore. He retired from the wrestling business and for twelve years now has given himself to serving in ministry, loving the Lord with all his heart, and loving people.

Now his mantra is "Hail, Jesus!"

A Guiding Voice from Heaven
Michelle Ralston's Story

My name is Michelle (Kinap) Ralston. I am a quarter Mi'kmaq. My grandmother, who is Indigenous, comes from a reserve called Bay Despoir, Newfoundland. My great-grandmother died at an early age and my great-grandfather was a fisherman. Although he loved his children very much, he had to give them to a white family so he could work. As a little girl, my grandmother was sexually abused by the people and would often hide in the cupboards or under the steps, hoping her father would return for her. My great-grandfather did return one day and took his children home.

I was the third child of my mother. My brother was the middle child, and he was given up for adoption. My mother didn't drink, but she often partied with people who did, and so my sister and I were in the way. When I was three, my mother took us to my grandmother's house. My grandmother told my sister she could stay, but I had to go with my mother. I could not stay. My little-girl heart felt very rejected and believed I did not belong. My mother took me to a home where I was sexually abused for six years. The spirit of rejection followed me for forty-five years.

When I was nine, I was taken back home and my father (who was a corporal in the Air Force) moved our family to West Germany from 1980 to 1984. I was fascinated by the history of the country, visited concentration camps and Anne Frank's house, and heard stories from survivors who escaped communism from behind the Berlin Wall. Their stories gripped me. I was alone a lot in our town off the base, so I spent my time running with horses across the street and climbing trees. I felt like God was always with me. I would talk to Him all the time. One day, He talked back—audibly—like a person in front of me. I was shocked and kind of scared but really curious.

I ended up winning first place in a dance contest during our last year in Germany and danced at a couple of orphanages. When we were stationed back to Canada, I remember feeling like I had landed on another planet. We arrived in Dartmouth, Nova Scotia, and I was immediately placed in a civilian school in north-end Dartmouth. There, I was befriended by girls in the school who were affiliated with a notorious gang called North Preston's Finest. They are known to be the biggest hubs of pimping and human trafficking in Canada. At thirteen years of age, my life got very confusing with these girls. I was often beaten up.

One day I was told to run for my life, because members of the NPF were coming to the school for me. I watched as they headed up the hill. My heart was in my toes! I ran deep into the woods and it took me hours and hours to get home. All I knew was they were known to have knives and guns and lies. They had accused me of being a racist. I was a sheltered little girl who did not understand the world she lived in. I tried turning to the police and my parents, but they didn't know how to respond to the situation.

I met an older girl who introduced me to another gang that took me under their wing, but eventually, the girl took me to a man's house where I was given Valium and was raped, sold, and then gang raped for a night. They sold me into human trafficking. I became addicted to Valium and continued to be trafficked willingly for the drug. I felt lost and desperately wanted to be numb.

For about a year—I really don't know how long—I just consumed acid, coke, Valium—any painkiller I could find. It led me to involvement with white supremacists. I didn't agree with their beliefs, but I was high enough not to care, and they wanted me. That year, I tried multiple times to commit suicide. One time, my sister found me just in time and repeatedly had to stick her finger down my throat until I was coherent.

When my mother and sister moved to British Columbia, I stayed living with my father in Nova Scotia. I was very neglected and wanted to tell someone what was happening, but I was too afraid, so I took downers and hung around my father, hoping he would ask questions, but to no avail.

At sixteen, I packed an army bag and, during a Nova Scotia blizzard, ran away from home to my mother in British Columbia. My boyfriend and I sold drugs for a Greyhound ticket and landed in B.C. in 1987.

I continued to drink and do drugs and found myself in horrible situations. I should have been dead, but I remembered my time with God in the field with the horses, and I would call out to Him, promising I'd change. Sometimes, I'd know it was Him telling me what to do to get away from danger, but it wasn't until I was twenty-five that I got clean and sober and began a journey of self-discovery.

With my four-year-old daughter, and having been a year and a half clean and sober, I discovered I was pregnant again. At the same time, my husband left to pursue another woman and his addiction again. All my "daddy" issues surfaced, and friends and family abandoned me. I felt broken into a million pieces. As I lay face down, sobbing into the carpet, I heard that voice again say, "I will never leave you." I was shocked. I kept hearing His voice as He pursued me and drew me closer. My only friend (who was a Christian) told me that the message I was hearing was Scripture. She gave me a Bible.

I had no idea what was going on within me, but I was changing. I didn't feel comfortable doing certain things anymore, like gossiping. I was so overwhelmed with love that on my birthday, I wanted to *give others* presents instead of *receiving* them. People thought I was nuts. I read the Bible for hours, day and night. I would hear God's voice tell me how much He loved me. I would walk outside, and the trees, birds, and wind would be singing to God. I fell in love with Jesus, and suddenly, I knew I had to be baptized, so I phoned my pastor on Wednesday, September 10, 1998, and said, "I have to be baptized tonight in the Coquitlam River." Poor guy, it was freezing, but I told him I'd do it myself if I had to. He actually honoured my excitement and came.

I used to wear provocative clothing, but that night, because I felt reborn and beautiful and pure, I took my entire wardrobe and threw it in the garbage. Then I went to the church garage sale and got a new wardrobe. Thank God, there were nice things there!

My husband went back into heroin and became very abusive, but God was always faithful. One night, it was as if Jesus hot-wired a car and threw my kids and me in, just in the nick of time. As we drove off, the tsunami of my husband's rage crashed just out of reach of our lives. Our last encounter with his abuse almost ended in tragedy. He tried to run down my third baby with his car, but we escaped into a remote place in the backwoods of Coquitlam.

Through all my trials, God was faithful. Along the way, God connected me with Pastor Randy and the First Nations Bible

College. I am so grateful because Randy was an amazing pastor, so encouraging, compassionate, and caring. He always made us feel like we were part of his family. I look forward to seeing him in heaven. I love him so much.

My Father in heaven is everything to me. He was the one who saved me. He was Jehovah Nissi—my protector. He was Jehovah Shammah, always present. I had nobody but Him. The church tried, but they didn't know what to do with me, so He was Jehovah Rohi, my intimate Shepherd. He was Jehovah Sabbaoth, the captain of my army. He was Jehovah Hoseenu, who created a way where there was no way. He was Elohim, my supreme sustainer, when I was on the road less travelled, full of prickle bushes and rough terrain. He gave me strength to go on. He was so faithful, so loving. He was my first love. He shocked me out of my limited thinking with every miracle. He dared me to believe Him for the impossible with healings no man can do and opening of doors no man can shut. He rocked my world so much that I fell back in His arms, and He became my Elohay, my ruler!

My new overcoming name that our heavenly Father gave me was Kinap, which is Mi'kmaq for "Brave Heart/ Warrior". This is who I am!

"I Am the One That Called You"
Poem by Michelle Ralston

Come, I have a story
I must tell to you today
A story 'bout a stranger
One of us? I cannot say.

One stormy morning
The stranger wakened from a dream
Pondering what he remembered
Got his coffee and his cream.

He headed to the river and got into his boat
Then once upon the other side
He knew not where to go ...
Without apparent guide.

Zipping up his leather
Scanning side to side
The forked road was narrow
The stranger must decide.

The wind was strong
The time was short, 11:59,
He made a choice to follow
For he didn't have much time.

Down along the narrow path
Someone called upon his name
Curious, he sought the voice
It must be a kind of game.

Her fragrance was sweet
Inviting him her way
He would not be disappointed
If he heard what she would say.

He stepped into her chambers
Like a capsule outside time
Shimmering beauty faced him there
With riches only prime.

The tick of time distracted him
To lure him from her way
Her hand reached out to reassure
Set time aside today.

He settled himself and turned to her
To hear what she would say.
Shunning, understanding,
He listened and marked the day!

She said, "Many ignore my call
And stumble across my way
They rarely make it past this point
With excuses they cannot stay."

Their ears are blocked and they don't hear
So quickly run astray
My son, you have an ear to hear
A heart to learn my way.

I'll give you understanding
And you will know the same
My son, draw near and listen close
WISDOM is my name.

Wear me like a garment
With my words held in your heart
Joy and laughter will be your reward
For I shall ne'er depart.

One day, you'll face Creator God
With choices you have made
Without me, you'll blame another
Nothing hidden or unsaid.

But wisdom is sweet medicine
Like incense 'round your home
My light shines bright in darkness
I'll guide you like a drum.

Feel the breath of the Great Spirit
Breathe Him in and you'll be ONE
He'll enlighten with understanding
The sweet mysteries of His SON

For He says:

I will not love and leave you
As many have done before
I came to free you from the trap
When sin walked through your door.

I was there, when it enticed you
To choose it, over me
The pain of separation,
You were never meant to see.

I AM the Good Shepherd
I AM the Rock that gave Moses water

I AM the manna from Heaven
I AM your Creator ... there is no other.

I AM the wind that compelled you
I AM the sweet and narrow road
I AM the voice that was calling
When direction was a load.

I AM the fragrance that drew you
To turn a different way
To give Me your disappointments
As you begin a brand new day.

I AM the chamber, I AM the place
I AM outside of time
I AM that shimmering beauty
I AM that humble pie.

I AM that understanding
If you take Me in your heart
I AM joy and laughter
I AM wisdom ne'er depart.

I AM sweet medicine
I AM incense in your home
When you allow My light to guide
No darkness dare abide.

I AM the drum
I AM the air you breathe
I AM the enlightened ONE
I AM the sweet mysteries.

I AM the SON.

The stranger gasped.
Falling to his knees
He touched the hem of His garment
While his tears fell to His feet.

The Father took him by the hand
And drew Him to His arms
Jesus lovingly pressed behind him
Holy Spirit wiped his tears.

Welcome home, you're not a stranger
We've been waiting a long time
See Our footprints next to yours
Stay close and you'll be fine.

Now go out into the world
With Our messages of love
We'll give you eyes of an eagle
Be wise and gentle as a dove.

He Skates and Scores!
Robin Sampson Jehu's Story

My name is Robin. I'm from Tsal'alh.

Tsal'alh is pronounced "Sha-LATH" in St'at'imcets, the Lillooet language. It means "lake" and refers in this case to Seton Lake, a freshwater fjord stretching twenty miles through a desert canyon, westwards from the Fraser River. Tsal'alh is a small, isolated First Nations community at the northern point of the St'at'imc Territory, sixty-five kilometres from Lillooet, B.C. Travel to and from the community is mainly by railway, alternating paved and dirt roads. In this remote area, I spent my childhood.

I first accepted Christ back when I was seventeen, but, having grown up in foster homes in a small town and having been tossed from one home to the next, I had developed an unstable foundation for my life. Consequently, I was up and down and fell away from God many, many times. I have had many good runs with the Lord, but now I'm back to stay.

I played a lot of hockey when I was a kid, and had a really good talent for it, even playing some elite levels. My dream was to go all the way to the NHL (like almost every young Canadian hockey player). However, when I got cut from the team, my dream was shattered and I took it really hard. I felt really lost, because I had thought playing hockey was what I was supposed to do with my life.

Thankfully, I had some Christian friends who were praying for me and cared about me. One day, I went for a walk and called out to God, "God, if You're really real, reveal Yourself to me!" Sure enough, God began to reveal Himself, but then I fell away, time after time.

So—fast forward to 2003. I was back home in my Indigenous community of Tsal'alh, B.C. I was serving the Lord on and off, but in reality, I was taking the call of God rather lightly.

I survived by working construction most of my adult life,

but that summer I had a restlessness stirring within me. I'd sit there on the couch, flipping channels in the evenings and finding little joy at work during the days. Nothing seemed to have any meaning for me. I was skating around the goalposts of my life, never able to do what needed to be done.

I know my prayer and devotion time was never long enough. I was too restless; but I believe that restlessness is one of the ways God calls us, because—deep down—I wanted to go deeper and take serving the Lord to the next level.

During those times, I was having conversations with Pastor Randy. He was encouraging me to go to Bible college. He began to minister to me about what he, as a leader, had seen in me. So I prayed and sought the Lord for another week, and I truly believe God was telling me to leave everything and step out in faith and go to First Nations Bible College. So I answered the call and took my relationship with Jesus to another level.

I'm proud to say I am hungry for the things of God and on fire for Him.

I am studying theology and developing spiritual giftings. I'm finding the greatest joy in serving the Lord, and my love for people is steering me in the direction to become a pastor. God has been to me Jehovah-Rapha, the Lord our Healer; and Jehovah-Shalom, the Lord our Peace.

Bullied, Beaten, and Blessed:
Evan's Breakthrough Story

I was born into a mixed heritage family with deep roots. My mother is First Nations and my father is German. In addition to my maternal grandmother being a Cree residential school survivor, my maternal great-grandfather was a Baptist minister.

From kindergarten to high school, I was bullied by friends and family. When I was in grade ten, I started to understand what happened to me in those early years. It was clear that my experiences were traumatizing, so a counselor referred me to a man who ran First Nations' sweat-lodge ceremonies.

In grade eleven, I started using drugs. One particular time, I stayed awake for seven days straight. As a result of extreme sleep deprivation, I experienced an induced psychotic episode. I woke up strapped to a stretcher in the hospital and I was never again the same.

Traditional Native medicines and ceremonies helped to stabilize my mind, but my psychosis, mixed with native spirituality, blurred my efforts to analyze my mind and circumstances.

One day, I went to a friend's church, and the Lord humbled me there. After comparing Native spirituality and Christianity with a pastor, my pride got the best of me. I took offense to something completely innocent that he said. I stormed out of the church, hating the God of the Bible. I exalted plants instead of God and even denied His existence.

But 2 Chronicles 7:14 says, "If my people, who are called by my name, will humble themselves and pray and seek my face and turn from their wicked ways, then I will hear from heaven, and I will forgive their sin and will heal their land." This truth was carved into my mind.

After some time, I came to my senses, apologized to the church elders, and was completely healed because of my confession of sin. The Bible tells us in James 5:16, "Confess your sins to each other and pray for each other so that you may be healed. The prayer of a righteous person is powerful and effective." After nearly nine years of Native spirituality, I decided to take a break from it. Within a year, I began a relationship with someone and she took me to church.

At this point in my life, I was okay with going to church because I had learned to respect the God of the Bible and had drifted away from the Native path. My friend took me to the evangelistic group, Alpha, where I received the Saviour through His Holy Spirit. Later on, I was baptized at my friend's house. Not long after that, a minister at the church shared, in front of the entire congregation, her open vision of me being a shepherd of the sheep and caring for the little ones.

After sharing my testimony of what God had done in my life, I enrolled in Bible college. My love for writing stories, teaching people and even drumming as a child helped me.

During my first year of Bible college, I wrote sermons. During my second year, I took up drumming on the worship team. I became very distracted from my calling as a preacher by joining a worship band for a few months. During the second half of my second year in Bible college, I decided to learn the top forty contemporary worship songs on Sunday afternoons, just a few hours before performing them live at Street Church.

However, I realized my opportunities in ministry would be very limited without a graduation certificate, so I left the band. I made the choice to not work, so that I could focus on graduation after two and a half years of Bible college. Attending school was not just about being on the worship team or writing sermons. It felt like God put me through a boot camp so I could grow and mature through numerous trials and tribulations. Through all of my experiences, I've discovered that everybody is naturally good at what the Lord has called them to do.

Healed of Hoarding Pain
Dayle Laboucane's Story

The rivers wouldn't sing if they took the rocks out!

My name is Dayle Vernon Laboucane. Dayle means "down in the valley"; Vernon means "bright, fun one"; and Laboucane means "smoking fish". It's a French name. I'm seven-eighths French and just one-eighth Native, but my Metis blood runs strong through my proud warrior spirit. My grandmother is a full-blooded Cree.

As a girl, my mother was raped. When I finally arrived in the world, she turned her head away from me and said, "Just take him away." She didn't even want to hold me. She just gave me up, without ever even looking into my eyes. Rejection was my first ever experience.

I was moved into a foster home with foster mom Hilda. Hilda had immigrated to Canada from England with no money. In twenty-six years, 150 foster children passed through her home. She taught us all in the old English way with sensible discipline and made sure we had three good meals a day, nice clothes, and a warm bed. When any challenges faced us, she taught us how to talk things out. She was stern and we respected her, but we knew she loved us. I'm thankful to have grown up with no abuse, no neglect, no violence, and no trauma. It was a safe environment.

We all loved Hilda and honoured her. It was a privilege to live under her roof. She was actually declared "Mother of the Year" while I was there. It was because of her that I have a level head and have been able to deal with the struggles in my life. I was the eldest. She considered me her son. It was an amazing, beautiful experience. We had wonderful times with so much fun together. I am so thankful for the old way of English disciplinary upbringing. The kids in her home were free to become the individuals we are.

My only real problem was at school. I noticed that all the Polish kids hung out with other Polish kids, the Italian kids with other Italians, and the Japanese kids with other Japanese kids. I used to walk home feeling that I didn't fit in anywhere because I didn't know what nationality I was. I had to wrestle with the insecurity of not knowing my heritage. For that reason, I was depressed and didn't like myself. I felt like I didn't really belong.

I stayed in the foster home until I was twenty-six years old. One night, when I was twenty-five, I cried out, "God, help me! I need Your help. Do You even exist? Are You even real?" I had grave doubts that there was any such thing as a divine being, but in my desperation, I called out.

The next day, I was talking with a cook at a local restaurant who wanted to talk about God. My answers were right there! I responded to the cook's efforts to reach out to me and gave God my heart and life. I got saved!

Then I started listening to Christian music. I would cry with every song I heard. I would sometimes write Scriptures out for eight hours at a time.

It was as if God would tap me on the shoulder and say, "Can I have this?"

I'd say, "Have what?"

God would say, "What's in your heart?"

Then I'd think of the dark things in my heart—things I harboured, and a lot of junk. I'd say to God, "But I like this junk! I'm a hoarder, I like to hold on to things!"

I had a lot of unforgiveness in my heart. When He brought people to mind, I'd say, "Really, God? I have to forgive them?" I got a picture in my mind of me pushing a big shopping cart with piles of unforgiveness spilling over the sides.

Finally, I gave everything to God—all those difficulties in my life, my insecurities, my feelings of not belonging anywhere, and the rejection that had welcomed me into the world. I cried away all my unforgiveness. The crying was hard; it was deep and overwhelming.

I think that many of us are so burdened down with the stuff going on in our heads and hearts that it's hard to walk in the freedom God offers. We hold on to so much from the past that we barely have room for the Holy Spirit. We all have dirty laundry that He wants to exchange.

When I made my exchange, I thought it would be difficult, but it was comforting. I just said, "Lord, here are my rags for Your riches."

Then I heard God say, "And now it is good to bless those people you've forgiven in your heart." My heart got cleaned out of all the bitterness, and He changed me so much that I started to want the best for the people I had to forgive. When I forgave, it was the best experience of my life.

Jesus died on the cross so I could forgive. I'm so thankful to Him for saving me and for forgiving my sins. When I confess my sin to Him, He is faithful to forgive me and cleanse me of whatever I've done or thought that was wrong. When you know the truth, the truth will set you free.

I have read the Bible for thirty-seven years. Through His Word, God showed me not to conform to the pattern of this world. He wants us to imitate Him! Jesus didn't preach theology. He taught through parables and word pictures. He was—and is—our tuning fork, helping us learn how we should tune ourselves to Him.

I met my real mom when I was forty. She had no affection for me. We had no history and therefore no real relationship. I make a conscious effort to not allow the pain of her rejection and the fact that she is a stranger to me stay inside. I refuse to let it take my joy away. The good thing about meeting her was that I learned a little bit about my heritage. Understanding my past and who I am helped me heal. It opened up my heart. Now I submit every thought to the Lord. I cling to His heart. My daily cry is that He will cleanse my heart and renew a right spirit in me. He's the lifter of my head.

For twenty-two years, I was married to a beautiful woman. She was sick most of those years, with headaches fifteen days out of thirty. She endured twelve years of headaches. Nevertheless, despite the headaches, she still had a heart to help other women, listen to them, and counsel them.

For eight years, she fought cancer. I tried to console and comfort her the best I knew how. I looked after her faithfully during that time. The last eight years were the most painful and long-suffering. As she lay dying, her sister and I held her hand and watched her pass away.

My wife thanked me for not leaving her when she went through the eight years of cancer treatments. I made a promise before God to stay with her until she died. I didn't want her to suffer by herself. I suffered with her and supported her to the end—not just for her, but because I have to stand before God and give an account to Him of what I do. I had such great respect for my wife. It was an honour to be married to her.

I, too, have struggled with issues. Being diabetic brings all kinds of complications to life. I've also lived through a motor-cycle accident. I worked in a shipyard sandblasting ships for thirty-seven years. I had a lot of bullying and trauma at work. I know what it's like to be pushed aside. But I know that Jesus went through a difficult time too.

When I found out about First Nations Bible College in Vancouver, I enrolled. It was an honour to study under Pastor Randy Barnetson. I learned to read God's Word and listen. Now I say, "Lord, show me something I need to change, someone I need to forgive. I will not harbour unforgiveness. You know my needs, Lord," and I give them to Him. I sit before Him quietly and submit every thought to Him.

Knowing that my grandmother was full-blooded Cree gives me great empathy with Native men. My heart goes out to them. I can see their hurt and pain of rejection. They have been traumatized. So many are dysfunctional. The history of strong Native warriors has been replaced by today's troubled men who have been hurt emotionally and are compromised in their lifestyles.

When God heals us from our pain, we develop empathy and a desire to help others experience the same freedom. When we are hurt so deeply and then experience healing, it actually becomes easier to identify others who are suffering with the same pain. Through our own pain, we develop compassion and a desire to help others embrace the true healing. My heart is to reach out and mentor Native men.

The Bible says a seed has to die before it grows. Jesus died on the cross. With Him in my heart, I grow. Jesus wants a loving relationship with us. He wants us to trust and follow Him.

I know what it is to pass from darkness to light. Jesus stepped in and dragged me out of miry clay. I traded my filthy rags for beautiful gifts—His love, His joy, His peace. Thank You, Jesus, for Yours is the kingdom, the power, and the glory forever and ever. Amen!

[On April 2, 2022, Dayle went home to be with his Lord Jesus Christ.]

Heavenly Martial Arts
Daniel Watkinder's Story

"Praise be to the LORD, my Rock, who trains my hands for war, and my fingers for battle" (Psalm 144:1).

I was raised in the Roman Catholic Church and because of this was required to attend religion classes at school. My Roman Catholic teacher said that we needed to know what Protestants believed. His goal was to teach us how to return these "fallen brothers" back into the fold, so he taught us what all the different denominations believed. Through his unfolding of Protestant beliefs, I discovered the truth, *God's* truth. My religion teacher's goal backfired, and at ten years old, I embraced this truth, the saving power of Jesus Christ, and I got saved.

"It is by grace you have been saved, through faith—and this is not from yourselves, it is the gift of God—not by works, so that no one can boast" (Ephesians 2:8–9).

"Jesus replied, 'Very truly I tell you, no one can see the kingdom of God unless they are born again'" (John 3:3).

These verses taught me that my salvation was just the beginning of my spiritual walk; and this is an ongoing process.

As a young boy, I developed a fighting exercise. In my twenties, I showed it to a martial artist. He said it could be useful against someone with a knife.

Little did I know the truth in his statement. Fifteen years later, it saved my life. I did not know at the time, but now I know it was God training me.

"He has delivered us from such a deadly peril, and he will deliver us again. On him we have set our hope that he will continue to deliver us" (2 Corinthians 1:10).

I was coming out of a store and saw a fight taking place. I didn't realize the perpetrator had a knife; then I saw that the other guy had been badly wounded, his guts hanging out of his stomach. As I turned, the attacker's knife struck me, puncturing my chest near my heart. My reaction of self defense due to my martial arts training was automatic. I immediately used the exercise God had showed me years before—and that's what saved my life!

"Praise the LORD, my rock" (Psalm 144:1)!

God Passes the Test
Jeffrey Hockley's Story

My name is Jeff, and I'm a grateful believer in Jesus Christ. I can honestly say that now; however, it was not always like that. Early on, I spent most of my time running away from God, right into the enemy's camp.

I was born into a broken home. My parents argued a lot and finally separated. To this day, my father does not recognize me as his son. He claims my mother cheated on him and got pregnant. According to her, that did not happen. Whatever happened, I was born into this broken world and born into sin. "All have sinned and fall short of the glory of God" (Romans 3:23).

"We know that we are children of God, and that the whole world is under the control of the evil one" (1 John 5:19).

So, yeah, growing up with a single parent really threw me off and I went off the rails. I got into drugs, alcohol, and sex at an early age. It took over my thinking, my actions, and my activities.

On the bright side, I was spiritual, in terms of knowing that we are not finite beings, but that there are eternal considerations. I understood that we don't just die once this body breaks down. I was interested in spiritual things, but I put my energy into studying Buddha, Krishna, nature, humanism, tarot reading cards, astrology, and many other things. I thank God He was patient and allowed me to go through all of that searching before I came to my final conclusion, that the answer is Christ—and Christ alone. The best love story ever told was that God Himself came in the flesh so that He could relate to humans. He was tempted by everything we are tempted with, and yet did not sin. Christ died for the world's sin and on the third day rose again. Praise God.

One day, I was asked to identify with a Bible character. I chose Gideon. Gideon was a timid ruler. In fact, when he's first introduced in the Bible, he's hiding from his enemies. Although he came from the least of the least in terms of tribes, he received a call from God to take on the Midianites, a huge, nomadic group of people who were depleting Israel's supplies. When Gideon heard he would be the one to save the Israelite people from their oppressors, he didn't really believe it at first. So he tested God. This—right off the bat—seems to contradict the command not to put the Lord to the test (see Deuteronomy 6:16). And Gideon tested God more than once. First, he asked God to put dew on a fleece he laid out, instead of on the ground. Then he asked for the opposite—a dry fleece and wet ground. Then—once more—the opposite. This whole exercise of testing came from a lack of faith. In the next part of the story, God pulled all the crutches out from under Gideon and forced him to rely on Him. When God told him to bring an army to take on the enormous Midianite army, Gideon assembled thirty-two thousand men. God dwindled the army down to three hundred. Gideon had no option but to rely on God for a miracle.

What I learned through this is:

1. God can work with a little bit of faith and God can work through anyone, even timid believers with little faith. A leader doesn't always have to be the boldest and most extroverted. God often works through believers who come from the least of the least, like Gideon. When we're hiding from what scares us most, God compels us to tackle it head on. But God wants us to trust Him.

2. God doesn't allow metaphorical crutches. Although He played along with Gideon's fleece tests, when it came to the actual battle, God refused to let Gideon have the comfort-cushion of a large army. The same happens in our lives when we rely

on cushions that offer us comfort. God put Gideon in a position where he had to rely on God for a victory.

We can hide for only so long before God pulls us out of our comfort zones to do His amazing work!

Catching Up with Destiny
Natalie Stevenson's Story

My name is Natalie. First of all, I want to thank the Lord Jesus for living in my heart and being my personal Saviour. I come from a line of pastors and am very blessed to have been brought up in the gospel of Jesus Christ. I'm the second eldest of six children. I have one older sister, two younger sisters, and two younger brothers. I was born on July 17, 1967, in a little town called Broadview, Saskatchewan, about 100 miles east of Regina, Saskatchewan. My grandfather on my dad's side is from the Cowessess First Nation in Saskatchewan. Both my father and my mother are from the Cree tribe.

I was born a sick baby with a brain tumor. The doctors told my parents, "You might as well accept that your baby girl, Natalie, is not going to live, so you should know she is going to die. If she does live, she won't be fully normal. She'll have slow learning disabilities and will need extra attention and care growing up, possibly for the rest of her life; so just give up and let her die. She'll have mental disabilities and be the odd child, different from her siblings."

By this time, my parents had already come to know Jesus as their personal Saviour and now were living for Him. They refused to listen to what the doctors told them, so they took me to a big tent meeting church service in Edmonton, Alberta, for prayer. The evangelist, Max Solbrekin, prayed over me and I was healed from the brain tumor that very night.

Later in my childhood, I started noticing that I was different from my brothers and sisters, looking like none of them or my parents. Feeling alone, I became a loner child, like I didn't belong in this family. I wanted to be loved and accepted like my siblings and my parents, but instead, felt rejected and not loved.

One day, when I was about four or five years old, we were at a camp meeting church service. I remember my paternal grand-father, Roger Stevenson, now deceased, calling my older sister, Jackie, and me to sing a song in the service. We did, and later, after we sang, my grandfather prayed over me and had a Word from the Lord: "This little girl, my granddaughter, Natalie, is going to be the singer of this family. God is going to use her to sing in the music ministry to win souls to Jesus. She will be anointed. She's got the voice. Many will be touched by her singing music ministry in the name of Jesus."

After my grandfather prayed that prophecy over my life, I knew then that I meant something to someone and that I was just as important and loved as my siblings. Thank You, Jesus, for showing how much You love me.

When the Lord called my parents to be evangelists, we trav-elled around during the summer months. My parents had a big tent to hold church services, and we would pull it around from reserve to reserve and state to state. We went to Alberta, Mani-toba, Saskatchewan, Ontario, and many states in the USA. I sang in church services wherever we went. It was a fun time, travelling around with my family. My dad plays guitar to this day.

At about the age of ten or eleven, I admired my dad's guitar playing and wanted to learn how to play, so I asked him to teach me some chords on the guitar. He taught my older sister and me the guitar and bass. A year later, I moved over to the bass with the help of my older sister, Jackie. I will forever be grateful for that.

At the age of fourteen, I tried alcohol for the first time. I liked the feeling it gave me, so I continued to drink for a few years. I ran away from home several times and my parents put me in a youth jail for runaways at the age of fifteen. I stayed there for about four months. When I turned sixteen, I left my home and started drinking again and got pregnant that year. I gave birth to my firstborn son, Christopher, on August 4, 1984, and fell back into alcohol for a short while. After I had Chris, I got pregnant with my second child, a little girl, and named her Heavenly. She was born on March 21, 1991. Again, I slipped back into alcohol for a short while, but then God started dealing with me.

One night, I went out drinking and ended up at a friend's house where we hung out and continued to drink. My friend and the other girl who was there (I didn't know her) ganged up on me and nearly ended my life that very night.

Early the next morning, hung over and a bloody mess, I called out the name of Jesus. I cried, "God, please get me out of here! Forgive me! I'm sorry!" As soon as I said those words, I knew that God heard my cry, and I was able to make my escape to freedom. The following Sunday, I went to the altar to repent and rededicated my life to Jesus. I was totally healed from that severe beating.

A year later, I asked the Lord to take my children and me away from Regina. I wanted to get away from my life of alcohol abuse because that was all I knew. So on Mother's Day, 1992, I packed a suitcase and went to Vancouver along with my kids and my boyfriend (my daughter's dad) and my best friend and her boyfriend. My relationship with my daughter's dad didn't last, because he took off back to Saskatchewan and left my kids and me in Vancouver.

I decided to stay and begin to put God first in my life. I prayed and said, "Okay, Lord, You brought me here. Show me what Your will is for me. I'm going to trust You to take care of me and my kids."

He spoke to me from John 10:27: "My sheep listen to my voice; and I know them and they follow me." So my kids and I lived in Surrey for two months. In August 1993, the Lord blessed us with a brand new three-bedroom townhouse in Burnaby, where we lived for ten years.

Suddenly, tragedy hit on the night of January 27, 2003. That Sunday night, my eighteen-year-old son, Chris, tragically passed away while I was at the Street Church service. It was a devastating blow for me and my daughter. It was the hardest thing I ever had to go through. No parent should have to bury their children at such a young age.

I knew there was no way out but to go to the Lord for strength and prayer. The people at Street Church stood by me through everything. It was there that I found my calling from the Lord as a worship leader—a fulfillment of my grandfather's prophecy from long ago.

I've been with Street Church for twenty-six years. The people there are still my church family. It's always been a blessing to be part of this ministry. It's a double blessing to have had Pastor Randy as my pastor. I learned so much from him and am very glad I got to minister and support his work for twenty-six years. I miss him dearly, but I know he's waiting for us in heaven. I am now a graduate of First Nations Bible College because I love the Lord. He has done so much for me, and I want all He has for me.

I've overcome addictions to alcohol, street drugs, and prescription drugs and have also been healed from painful rejection. I wanted to give up so many times, but the Lord was faithful. He is on my side.

In a conversation I had with my dad, I asked him, "If you were to give me your final words, what would they be?"

He said, "Just keep serving and trusting the Lord. Keep singing for Him. He came to save us. I'll see you on the other side."

I, Natalie Stevenson, want to proclaim that I'm here by the grace of God and I know He has a plan for me.

Chapter 5

Hotdog Church and Healing Hands

A Tribute to Randy Barnetson
A True Leader

Pastor Randy Barnetson was saved during the Jesus People movement. He went to Bible college and was the youngest in his class to graduate. With an amazing heart for those struggling with homelessness and addictions, he pastored throughout B.C. and on the reserves, taking the message of the love of God wherever he saw pain and affliction.

In the early morning hours of Friday, October 9, 2020, after a prolonged battle with diabetes and kidney failure, he passed on to be with the Lord. His name is legendary on the cold, hard streets of downtown Eastside Vancouver, where his loss remains an ache in the heart of the community.

Who was this man, Randy Barnetson, who cared so deeply about the people on the street that he put their needs ahead of his own?

In a conversation I had with him before he died, Randy said, "I pastored up north and all around B.C. on Native reservations. That's where I got a love for First Nations people. I ended up here in Vancouver, wanting to plant a church.

"I was driving a school bus at the time. One morning, I had it parked out in front of my place. I got up early and was shocked to see a dead body in front of my bus on the ground. I freaked and called the police. They came by and just looked at the body. It was a woman. They covered her over with a sheet and then started talking about the hockey game. They looked at me and could tell I was visibly shaken, but said, 'It's okay; she was just a drug addict.'

"God powerfully spoke to me through that experience. I knew I wasn't to have my church in some nice neighbourhood in Vancouver, but that I should go down to East Hastings Street.

"The church has been here for twenty-five years in this location. Street Church is affectionately called the 'Hot Dog Church.' Since 1995, we've given out more than one million hot dogs. It's a place where people can come in and feel safe and get some food. At the front we have music playing and people sharing testimonies. Afterwards, I'll share something from the Word as well. It's like a church, but not a regular church.

"What I saw when I travelled across the land was that a lot of reservations have churches, but they're typically pastored by non-Indigenous people. There are seven hundred First Nations communities across Canada and many opportunities to church plant. Obviously, the best leadership for a First Nations church is a First Nations person.

"First Nations Bible College is an inner-city program. Even though we present the same material that they do in a regular Bible college, we offer free tuition. It's the only way most of these students could attend, and the only way we can fulfill our goal of providing First Nations pastors for First Nations churches.

"Our goal at the Bible college is to train leaders—pastors, evangelists, church planters, and missionaries—to reach every one of the one thousand First Nations communities, reservations, and settlements in the USA and Canada. So far, I have personally visited over six hundred Indigenous communities.

"Besides serving as the director of First Nations Bible College, I also serve as the pastor at Vancouver Foursquare Church, known as Street Church, in the downtown Eastside area of Vancouver.

"We have served over one million homeless and addicted people on the streets in the nation's poorest neighbourhood over the past twenty-five years. Our church meets Sundays, Wednesdays, and Fridays at seven p.m. at 175 East Hastings Street in Vancouver. I've been here for twenty-five years, and they'll have to carry me out feet first. I just love it here and I love working with people."

I asked Randy every year, "What is the prophetic word for this year?"

He always said, "Pretty much the same as last year: visit the prisoners, clothe the naked, feed the hungry, do justice, love mercy, walk humbly with God."

"Jesus answered, 'It is written: "Man shall not live on bread alone, but on every word that comes from the mouth of God"'" (Matthew 4:4). Randy's Bible college students helped feed hundreds of people and were committed to studying and sharing God's Word and making disciples.

During the Covid-19 pandemic, Randy was on the front lines, taking "Street Church" to the sidewalk, ministering where the people were. From his wheelchair, Randy would extend a broomstick with a rubber glove on the end to "lay hands" on people to pray for them.

My friend Becky Thomas, who was invited with me to teach at Randy's First Nations Bible College, remembers Randy with these words: "It was sometimes joked that if one left Randy Barnetson alone in a desert with not a soul to be seen, in twenty minutes he would be sitting with at least one local, introducing them to Jesus. This actually happened on a mission tour down south when the mission bus left without him. It was a good twenty minutes before the team realized Randy was missing in action. When they returned to get him, sure enough, there was Randy sitting with a local, although there was no one else to be seen for miles!

"When Randy walked the streets of Vancouver, the homeless who camped on the streets on East and Hastings streets would call and reach toward him, their faces transformed with the joy at seeing their friend and pastor. The bond of kinship formed in such difficult circumstance was a beauty to behold.

"Randy was a great encouragement to me as I first began to experiment with my Native sound," said Becky. "Every time I would release a song, he would call to encourage me. He was also musical. One day, I walked up the steps to Street Church and was excited to hear a great new Country Gospel band playing. When I arrived at the top, lo and behold, it was Randy taking the lead with First Nations Bible College students. It became clear that Randy could have successfully made his own albums—and maybe even have had a music career—but instead, he chose to play in the background to support other Native musicians. He only came to the forefront when there were no other lead singers available. Ironically, while we would have listened to his music all day, he chose instead to listen to ours."

Becky continued: "One day, I confided in Randy's beautiful Native wife some insecurities around my Native roots. The family I come from is very fragmented, so much so that I have been left with no paperwork to legally claim status. Having been told that we had Native blood flowing on both sides of our family, I felt pretty confident in stepping into my identity as a mixed blood (Caucasian and Cherokee). This was something that I was starting to do in faith, feeling led by the Lord to do so. That said, I have become acutely aware of the political and social implications of blood quantum. On my mother's side, the bloodline came into question. As this felt so devastating, I poured out my heart to Cheryl. She must have told Randy, because a few weeks later I got a phone call.

"Randy gave me a brief greeting and then launched into a pep talk that felt very much like a lecture. He expressed how rude it was for people to ask what percentage of blood one was, pointing out that nobody ever asked how German he was. He deemed those types of questions very inappropriate. He then exhorted me to be confident as a First Nations woman, to not back down or apologize, or allow politics to rob me of my identity and what I know to be true. With no further discussion, he hung up and I was left staring at the phone and wondering what just happened!

"I hold Randy up with the greatest esteem. To me, he is what a true missionary looks like—a coach who gives everything to his client and then moves out of the way. Randy provided a structure and a platform for Native people, and really for all people. When we had what we needed, he moved out of the way so we could succeed.

"I don't know if I have ever met anyone like Randy Barnetson, or will ever meet one like him again. I can say that he was truly the most humble and giving person I have ever met, and was possibly the most committed. He literally chose to live a life of poverty, and gave up personal privacy. He had this all-out commitment to ministry and to the people he served.

"I don't know enough to really comment on Randy's personal life, but I know that his sons, his friends and co-leaders loved him dearly. Vancouver and the Indigenous world have lost a great friend in Randy Barnetson."

Chapter 6

The First Native-Led House of Prayer

By Carmen Jones

My name is Carmen Jones and I am Ojibway. My parents are both Ojibway. My grandmother on my mother's side is Delaware, from the Delaware Nation in Moraviantown, Ontario. My grandfather on my mother side is Ojibway from Cape Croker, Ontario.

I am from the Wolf Clan. I live three hours north of Toronto, Ontario. My community has three names. The English name is Cape Croker, while the Ojibway name is Neyaashiinigmiing, which in our language means "Land Surrounded by Water". Our people are the Chippewas of Nawash. This explains my background and my heritage, but, most important, I am a son of God.

I am the leader of the Nawash House of Prayer. I am told that this is the very first Native-led and Native-run House of Prayer in Canada. The Nawash House of Prayer is here for anyone to come to worship and pray. In light of the recent residential school discoveries of unmarked graves, we have been asked to go to churches to speak and educate the public about the legacy of trauma of residential schools.

I would love to share my heart with you on this subject because through the residential schools, the government stole much more than our childhoods, families, and (sometimes) our lives. The understanding of spiritual things was twisted by the terrible things the church did in the name of Jesus. We have been robbed of the understanding of who Jesus *really* is.

The name of Jesus means so many things to so many different people in Canada and also in the world. To some this is the name above all names. It is the name that, when spoken, makes the enemy flee. Unfortunately, to some, the name of Jesus or God causes pain or hate to well up inside. It feels hurtful and destructive because, through the residential schools, Jesus wasn't presented the way He presented Himself. The *real Jesus* touched, healed, and changed people's lives—just through His presence and His name.

So why do people have this view of a hurtful Jesus?

In Canada, many of my Native brothers and sisters associated the name of Jesus with the horrible abuses they experienced in residential schools, Indian day schools, religion, colonization, and assimilation, as well as through institutions or organizations within their own communities. Many have been shown a counterfeit Jesus.

With the recent discovery of many young children found secretly buried at residential schools, many have questioned the part Jesus and Christianity played in the horrors. They have questioned whether there are any benefits to Christianity—whether it's even good. These children died at the hands of people professing to know Jesus, professing to follow God, and professing to teach and raise them to know Jesus.

As we all know (now), residential schools were institutions that housed children who had been stolen from their homes. The children were physically and sexually abused and some even killed. Now questions are being asked by all kinds of people—those who know Jesus, those who think they know Him, and many who do not know Him; but it's the same question: "Why did this happen?" Many go on to ask, "Is this what God or Jesus is all about—killing young children?"

Sadly, many Native and non-Native people both in Canada and throughout the world associate Him with horrors because of many evil things that have been done in His name. I am writing this in hopes of confirming 100 percent that the *real Jesus* is totally opposed to sexual abuse and stealing children from their parents. Most important, the *real Jesus* is not about killing young innocent children. He came to bring life—not death!

Nevertheless, this has been a struggle for so many people. One of the very first Christian songs I learned was "Jesus Loves Me." The lyrics are simple, but true:

Yes, Jesus loves me,
Yes, Jesus loves me,
Yes, Jesus loves me,
The Bible tells me so.

As Christians, we are supposed to *be like* Jesus in every way. We also should *want* to be like Jesus in every way. In the Word (the Bible), Jesus offers protection for children. In Matthew 19:14, Jesus said, "Let the little children come to me, and do not hinder them, for the kingdom of heaven belongs to such as these." Jesus loved children and invited them to "come to Him". This is completely different than what happened at the residential schools, where children were kidnapped and forced to learn about the counterfeit Jesus.

Let me illustrate how the counterfeit Jesus was presented to my Native brothers and sisters. It will also illustrate who the *real Jesus* is.

Suppose I showed you a $100 bill. What is it? Some would say one hundred dollars; some would say a good amount of money, and some would say a hundred bucks. How do we know it's one hundred dollars? For some, it's because of the color. If it was in your hands right now, you might say it's because of the texture or because it smells like maple syrup. How do you know it's real?

Are you a bank teller? Do you work at the Canadian mint? The answer is usually "No, I just know that this is a hundred Canadian dollars."

Now suppose I drew a hundred-dollar bill by hand and showed it to you. You would know it's fake, but I pretend that this is one hundred dollars. I included "Canada" and "100 bucks" so there's no question. I even drew a man on there—yes, it is a stick man, but it's still a man, right? This hundred-dollar bill even says, "I'm real (I swear)." It is even giving you a guarantee! It is so fake that it's laughable.

This illustration represents how Jesus, God, and the gospel were presented to my people. They were introduced to a *counterfeit Jesus*. The second example, the counterfeit bill, represents residential schools, religion, physical abuse, sexual abuse, colonization, assimilation, and man-made rules. *None of these represent the true character of Jesus!* Nevertheless, this is how my people were shown Jesus. No wonder our communities are so broken.

But the genuine currency represents the *real Jesus!* This is the Jesus who is all about love, joy peace, patience, kindness, goodness, faithfulness, gentleness, and self-control. This is the *real Jesus*, who died for our sins! This is the Jesus revealed and presented through the power of the Holy Spirit. We can no longer introduce people to Jesus through religion, rules, or our own efforts. We have to rely 100 percent on the Holy Spirit.

Zechariah 4:6 says, "'Not by might nor by power, but by my Spirit,' says the LORD Almighty."

Second Corinthians 3:17 states, "Where the Spirit of the Lord is, there is freedom."

So when we know the Word of God (the Bible), we can see and recognize who the *real Jesus* is and who the *real God* is. Most important, we can truly know Jesus and God only through the power and revelation of the Holy Spirit.

In John 16:14, Jesus says, "[the Holy Spirit] will glorify me because it is from me that he will receive what he will make known to you." Therefore, the Holy Spirit's job is to reveal Jesus.

That being said, we can do only what the Holy Spirit is leading us to do. Anything else is human effort. Strategy, ministry, church events—and even church—are all examples of what can be considered human effort *unless* they are *completely led by the Holy Spirit.*

One of the reasons why residential schools were able to happen was because some people, *out of their own efforts,* thought they had a good idea about how to bring Native people to Jesus. This is where the delusion started. But what actually happened was that these man-made ideas drove many *further away* from Jesus than they ever were before.

The Word says that when Jesus told the disciples that He was going to be crucified, Peter actually rebuked Jesus and exclaimed, "Never, Lord! This shall never happen to you!" Jesus then turned to Peter and said, "Get behind me, Satan! You are a stumbling block to me; you do not have in mind the concerns of God, but merely human concerns" (Matthew 16:21–23).

We cannot begin to strategize or minister without the Holy Spirit, because if we do, we are just doing this through human effort or "concerns". This is how we bring the real Jesus to our Native brothers and sisters, and anyone else who does not know Him: through the power and leading of the Holy Spirit.

It was because of the deep traumas that happened over the many generations to our First Nations brothers and sisters that we started the Nawash House of Prayer. We want to see people set free. We also want to show people who the *real Jesus* is. We want them to understand that the person who was presented in the residential schools was not the *real Jesus who loves them and died for them.* The *real Jesus* is full of love, patience, kindness, and grace for them.

To all of my First Nations, Inuit, and Metis brothers and sisters, and anyone who has been shown a false Jesus, I urge you to open your hearts to the *real Jesus!* He's calling you. He loves you just as you are. Sit and spend time with Him. He will not hurt you. There is safety in the presence of the *true Jesus*. He wants to fill you with His love. He wants give you His peace. He wants to heal you of your past hurts and traumas. He wants to strengthen you in your spirit. He wants to restore joy and laughter in your life. Jesus is on *your* side. Jesus loves you *so much!*

Chapter 7

Moccasin Identifier Initiative

Carolyn King's Story

One of the amazing women of our time, Carolyn King, is the initiator of the Moccasin Identifier Initiative. Initiating and developing ideas and plans to deepen the understanding and positioning of her people, not only through history but also today and through all the tomorrows of time, she is a true visionary. In her words, we introduce her Moccasin Identifier Initiative.

"Ahnii / Hello, my name is Carolyn King, née MacDonald. I am a member of the Mississaugas of the Credit First Nation, located in Southern Ontario. I was born on the Six Nations of the Grand River territory, an Iroquois/Haudenosaunee community. My mother was a residential school survivor from the Mohawk Institute in Brantford and my father was a farmer and ironworker. I am the third child of eleven. As a large family, we lived our entire lives on the reserve.

"I married Fred King, a member of the adjacent Mississaugas of the Credit First Nation, and I became a member and resident there. We were married for fifty-three years and had two children and now have five grandchildren. Fred passed away in the spring of 2021.

"I worked for the First Nation as a community economic development worker and was consistently involved in marketing and promotional activities over the eighteen years I was an employee there. My many volunteer activities include planning the annual cultural event, establishing and managing the public library, and the local Indigenous community radio station. I saw the need to educate and make the surrounding communities aware of our nation and people, so I participated fully in First Nation outreach activities.

"As a former elected chief of the Mississaugas of the Credit First Nation, I was the first woman ever elected as their chief. I held office from 1997 to 1999. For over thirty years, I worked with communities, organizations, educational institutions, and government agencies to give a voice to Indigenous and First Nations groups.

"I call myself the creator of the initiative called the Moccasin Identifier. The Moccasin Identifier was developed to educate people about the history of Indigenous peoples' treaty lands and traditional territories, and to help people recognize and honour places of significance.

"The project was born out of a simple but powerful idea. In places that are significant to Indigenous people, an image of a moccasin is stenciled on the ground. The fact that the paint and stencils are not permanent is part of the uniqueness of the project. Permanency is planned not in indelible ink, but in the incorporation of the project into school programs as an annual stenciling event to represent those who have come and gone but 'left no mark.' The unique stenciled designs of moccasins, applied with washaway paint, are a continuous reminder of the treaty and traditional lands.

"It is my hope that the initiative will grow nationally to the point that all of Canada will be covered in moccasins to remind everyone of the mark we and others leave on the land.

"The Moccasin Identifier evolved out of a digital mapping project that First Nations was supporting. The idea was that communities, using technology, could mark their sites of significance and tell their stories. People would use their smartphones to tap on a dot on an interactive map and Indigenous information would come up about the area. Also, significant sites would be identified to inform municipalities—and developers—before development projects started. They would be able to see why a particular site was important to Indigenous people and why it shouldn't be disturbed, or how the plans could be modified to meet the needs of Indigenous people. The washaway paint stenciling program was born from this idea of the digital mapping project. It was essentially a move from digital to physical. However, there is a plan to somehow incorporate a digital dot on the stencil, possibly a QR code, which people could access on their phones to scan for information about the website.

"As the project develops, people will be able to see what is important on these websites; such as village sites, trails, seasonal camps, or burial sites.

"The educational component focuses on elementary grade levels, with a kit that contains the stencils and tools for using them in school curriculum. We are now broadening the audience to all who may be interested in learning about Indigenous peoples of this country. In the decade of developing and promoting what is now called the Moccasin Identifier, we have presented at hundreds of events and to thousands of school children. The website for the initiative is www.moccasinidentifier.com.

"I have been honoured with several awards, including receiving an eagle feather from my community and, in December of 2020, being appointed to the Order of Canada. An eagle feather is one of the Anishinaabe's highest honors and compares to Canada's high order. I can now joke about having both honours. I believe we can preserve our history and the world can be changed, 'one moccasin at a time.'"

Chapter 8

River of Healing

Saskatchewan Log Church,
Onion Lake First Nation[1]

I, Belma, received an invitation to take the "River of Healing" to the Log Church at Onion Lake First Nation in Saskatchewan. I was to be the keynote speaker for the First Nations Ladies' Conference. The River of Healing is a ministry tool with which God equipped me several years ago. To explain its power, let me go back a bit.

I had been going to revival meetings in the days of the Toronto Blessing and always wanted to be right in the middle of whatever it was that God was doing. Seeing Him work in such profound ways in lives was overwhelming. I couldn't stay away. I didn't want to miss anything. It was amazing.

One night, when the Lord was ministering to me there, I felt a beautiful presence come over me and I fell to the floor like silk. I lay there for three hours. My physical body felt unable to get up. As I rested, I seemed to be walking in a lush green pasture, hand-in-hand with Jesus. We came to a river and He told me it

1. A very special thank you to my beautiful sister-in-the-Lord and fellow traveller, Beverly Hadland, Ambassador to First Peoples at Crossroads Christian Communications Inc., who flew with me and was a tremendous support and encouragement, organizing and facilitating every aspect of this entire ministry trip—caring for all my needs, lending a helping hand wherever needed, and praying faithfully. Special thanks to Teresa Matos-Telo, also from Crossroads, who accompanied us to pray.

was the river of healing, which flowed from the throne of God (see Revelation 22:1). The first part of the river was very shallow, about a foot deep. As we walked farther into the river, I noticed the water flowing through my leg, not around it. We continued to walk, and a refreshing feeling flowed through my body, from my toes up to my head.

After the three hours, I struggled up and had to be driven home. Early the next morning, at two a.m., I suddenly awakened and, upon opening my eyes, heard a voice say, "Look at your leg."

Ever since July 1988, I had a growth on my leg. It had started out as a rash, but by March 1994, it was about four inches long and two inches wide, raised to about a sixteenth of an inch. It was extremely irritating, itchy, and painful. Over the years, doctors told me it was a skin condition I would have for life. They could do nothing for me.

I knew immediately to look where the growth had been. It was totally gone! I gasped and touched the spot, rubbing it in awe. It was so smooth, it looked like brand new skin. I thought, *I must be dreaming!* "Where did it go, Lord?" I asked in amazement. "What happened?" Eventually, I fell back to sleep.

When I awoke later that morning, it was still healed. It hadn't been a dream! I marvelled at the healing and found it very hard to digest that God would love me so much as to heal me.

That night I had a dream in which I relived the entire experience of the previous night. As I lay on the church carpet, I again walked in heaven, hand-in-hand with the Lord. We came to the river and He said, "This is the river of healing. In it there is healing. As we were walking through it, you were healed. My child, I love you; receive My love." At that moment, I woke up, weeping. Little did I know that this river would become the vehicle of healing for thousands in Indigenous communities and in conference settings around the world.

God refers to the moving of His Spirit like the flowing of a river. We feel it as it fills our hearts with warmth and love. Where there was despair, there is new life and hope. This is the river that flows to us directly from God.

Some time later, God lead me to purchase fifty metres of fabric to replicate a river in a building. People could gather around it and walk through it to find healing for their bodies and souls.

Alvina Thunderchild, in whose generational line are many chiefs, comes from the line of Chief Morningchild, and her husband, Fred, from the line of Chief Thunderchild. They reside on the Thunderchild reservation outside of Turtleford. When she heard I was going to Onion Lake with the River, she drove two hours with her four grandchildren to the Log Church. She and I were overjoyed to see each other again. We had met a few days prior at a conference and had connected immediately as though we'd been lifelong friends. In our first moment of meeting, she removed her scarf and placed it around my neck.

The first night at Log Church, I shared how my mother had tried to abort me and how I had been ripped from the loving care of my grandparents to suffer a life of horrible abuse with my mother (see my first book, *Because God Was There*). I then invited people to walk through the River of Healing. They couldn't get there fast enough. They pushed and pressed in to make their way to the symbolic river of God's healing love. They couldn't wait to walk through it.

A little nine-year-old boy, Brandon, and his grandmother were two of the first to walk through. The little boy suddenly jolted to a stop and cried out, "Grandma! He's real! He's real! Jesus is real!"

The words flew out of his mouth like lightning, confirming what we were all feeling in the depths of our souls—the enveloping presence of Jesus wrapping His arms around each precious one, bathing us in the light of His glory. There was no doubt in our minds that God was with us. He was real.

Alvina turned to her four grandchildren and said it was time to forgive their mother, Chasity, for killing herself. In a huddle, arms around one another, one gradual step at a time, they walked very slowly through the River of Healing and were able to release her to the Lord. At the end of the River of Healing there is a "lake", where they sat for a very long time, facing the cross, sharing intimate moments together with Jesus as a family. Forgiveness flowed and they were set free!

The worship team began to play, and a beautiful thing happened. The children got up and started to move with the rhythm of the music. Others joined them, and spontaneous dance broke out with an anointing of supernatural breakthrough for healing of emotions.

Originally, Pastor Martin of the Log Church and his wife had booked to go away that weekend for personal time, but the Lord had told them to stay, allowing his wife to attend the ladies' conference. Then Pastor Martin heard from the Lord himself, "*You* go to the ladies' conference too!"

"Not only did God touch the ladies, but He touched me," he said. "There was a release and a healing that happened inside my spirit—but not only in my heart. It happened physically! I couldn't believe how energized I felt! An amazing new freedom. God really touched me physically and emotionally. I really need-ed it. I'm sure I received just as much as the women did."

A woman named Bernice said, "I was able to forgive people who hurt me."

Linda Naistus said, "A lot of healing came when I walked through the River of Healing. It washed away my brokenness and deep pain. All the garbage within me was washed away and I felt much freer to worship."

One after another, stories came of Jesus healing and eras-ing deep wounds in people's lives as they walked through the symbolic River of Healing.

When everyone had walked through the River of Healing, a great sense of freedom and peace pervaded as we shared not only a meal together, but also stories of how God had nurtured each soul.

"The Lord is the Spirit, and where the Spirit of the Lord is, there is freedom" (2 Corinthians 3:17).

"The LORD gives strength to his people; the LORD blesses his people with peace" (Psalm 29:11).

Chapter 9

Thunderchild First Nation

Two weeks after the First Nations Ladies' Conference, Alvina Thunderchild invited me [Belma] to go to the Thunderchild First Nation with the River of Healing. She wanted the same freedom for her people on Thunderchild First Nation that she had seen at Onion Lake. She said, "My people need to be healed from past hurts. The whole community needs to come and walk through the River of Healing."

Like most First Nations communities, the Thunderchild First Nation has suffered a tragic history. The ripple effect of tragedy after tragedy has washed ashore and beached the lives of ongoing generations.

November 27, 1885, marked the day of the largest mass hanging in Canadian history, an example of the subjugation of Indigenous peoples under British colonialism. Two decades later the area became part of the Canadian prairie provinces, where waving wheat graces hundreds of miles of flat, golden fields.

But that day, in 1885, eight Cree warriors were hanged at Fort Battleford, Saskatchewan, for their role in the North-West Rebellion. The horror echoed similarities to the largest mass execution in the United States, following the Dakota War of 1862. These were the bloody years of colonialism. The Canadian executions followed the North-West Resistance, the Frog Lake Massacre, and the looting of Fort Battleford.

The North-West Resistance had sprung up as a response to the Canadian government's sale of lands and consequent outlawing of centuries-old traditions of self-support, such as buffalo hunting. The result was starvation, disease, and death among Indigenous peoples of the area.

The men who were hanged were Indigenous warriors who knew nothing of the new Canadian legal system. They were strangers to concepts of lawyers and legal counsel. For them, justice had always been sought through tribal traditions and rules. These new Canadian laws over their own lands were as foreign to them as were those of foreign countries. Without representation, they had no defense. Sir John A. MacDonald had been very public about his policy of keeping the Indians as close as possible to starvation. Indian Agent Thomas Trueman Quinn maintained hardline enforcement of that policy and treated the Cree with harshness and arrogance.

At both Frog Lake and Fort Battleford, in desperation, some of the people armed themselves, against the wishes of their leaders.

Before dawn on April 2, 1885, some Cree warriors captured Quinn at his home. They attempted to take him to another location, but when he refused to go with them, he was shot and killed right there, the first to be killed at Frog Lake. In the ensuing panic, eight other settler prisoners were also shot and killed.

While some of the warriors managed to flee to the United States, the eight who were captured faced trial on charges of murder. Conviction would mean hanging. With no defense, it was as good as done before the trial even began.

The captives were taken to Fort Battleford, where there was a trial heard by Battleford "Resident Stipendiary Magistrate" Judge Charles Rouleau, whose house had been burned to the ground during the rebel looting. He reportedly threatened that every rebel brought before him would be sent to the gallows if possible. When the gavel was pounded and the verdict proclaimed, the Cree-speaking men who were sentenced to hang were provided with no translation regarding their fate.

There are a number of first-hand historical records from settlers and student witnesses of the hangings. Those were also the days of the horrendous experiments in cultural bleaching through residential schools.

All the students from the Battleford Industrial Residential School were marched to the town square to watch the hanging. The idea was to remind them what would happen to anyone who made trouble, and to engrave an unforgettable reminder of white man's power and authority on their minds.

Not surprisingly, the trauma was so great that one of the boys decided to burn down the residential school. He and his friends whispered a plan. They told the other children to keep their clothes on one night. They did. When the boys lit the school on fire, all the children escaped and hid in the forest. Of course, the government found them quaking and shivering in the underbrush and the outcome was not good.

After the closure of that school, many Indigenous children from around Battleford were sent to various schools in Saskatchewan, including Thunderchild Residential School in Delmas.

According to Alvina, "We, the generations, have been affected by this, causing a lot of suicides, and we need healing."

Six months after Alvina's invitation to take the River of Healing to Thunderchild First Nation, I was all packed and ready to go. Fifty pounds of blue material for the River of Healing was folded in my suitcase.

Then I received a text from Alvina. "There might be a funeral this week."

A twenty-year-old Native boy, Nelson (name changed for anonymity), a member of a gang, had been murdered in Edmonton. After a number of weeks, his body had been found. It was now being held in police custody. When the investigation was finished, the authorities would be moving the body from Edmonton to Thunderchild First Nation. They planned to have the funeral in the community hall where the River of Healing was to be held.

I immediately felt uncomfortable to take the River of Healing there. How could I ask people to walk through it when this murder and their grief was so fresh? I called Alvina and shared my concerns, suggesting they not have me speak. Since my flight was booked, I said I would go anyway just to walk alongside the people and serve them during their time of grief.

Alvina spoke with the family about my thoughts and concerns. They decided that the ladies' conference should still happen, but at the church adjacent to the community centre, rather than at the community centre itself. The two buildings shared the same parking lot.

The day I flew in was the same day the body arrived in Thunderchild. Alvina and I decided to go and pay our respects.

When we arrived at the community centre, one of the grandmothers was standing outside to greet us. A van drove up and I was introduced to the boy's mom, who fell into my arms wailing. "They murdered my baby. They shot him! They burned him! I want my baby back. I don't know how to help myself." Her grief was gut-wrenching.

We went into the hall and paid our respects amid the hushed tones of helplessness and sorrow.

The deceased had been in one of the most dangerous and powerful gangs from a far-off city. When we entered the hall, we saw all the gang members dressed in their full colours standing in a circle. It was as if God pulled Alvina and me into that circle and sent us to fearlessly shake the hands of every gang member, offering our compassionate condolences. When we approached them in this non-threatening way, each of them instantly opened their hearts to us. At that moment, we felt that relationship and trust were established.

Afterward, we went to the church and started the ladies' conference. When the ladies' meeting was done for that evening, we went back to the hall to visit with the family and gang members.

Weeks before, Alvina had told the grandma about my book, *Because God Was There*, and upon her request had given the grandma two copies. Now they were requesting more copies, enough for everyone. Apparently, the grandma had shared the story with the family and gang members.

As Alvina talked to the gang members, she pointed to me and said, "You see Belma? That's her story. She's with us today."

The gang members replied, "This is so cool."

We left another dozen books with them. With heartfelt thanks, they all said it would give them something to read during the wake while they sat beside their brother Nelson's coffin throughout the night.

The funeral would be the next day.

The Funeral

When we arrived at the funeral, some of the family came running to us and said, "Please, can we have more books? We read your book to Nelson last night. We got to chapter 4. We were all crying."

Alvina and I looked at each other. I had brought books to give away at the ladies' conference, but with this request we left another full box. The family members put the books on a table at the end of the casket for everyone to help themselves.

We then asked if we could help in the kitchen. We were sent to ask the grandma who was outside, sitting by the fire. She said, "Yes, we need help."

"What would you like us to do?" we asked.

She shrugged her shoulders. "What can you do?"

Alvina pointed to me and said, "She can preach."

I pointed to Alvina and said, "She can sing."

The grandma said, "Okay. Good. That's what you'll do."

We asked her who was in charge that we should talk to.

"No one is in charge. Now you are in charge. You will do the funeral."

We were stunned. We had no time to waste! We ran and grabbed Alvina's guitar and prayed under our breath as we sat waiting in the hall, enveloped by the sounds of the tormented, piercing cries of the mourners. The wailing bounced back and forth, echoing off all four corners of the building.

The elders motioned for us to start the service. We didn't know what we were going to say, but God led the way.

I shared Scriptures of comfort and talked about heaven. Alvina sang a song of love from the Creator, and together, we sang "Amazing Grace". The atmosphere changed. It was like a beautiful, thick comfort cloud was lowered from the heavens to rest on the people. We ourselves felt gripped by this heavenly presence as well. We talked about how we knew someone personally who had been beaten and murdered just like their brother and how His Father had to watch the torturous murder of His own Son. His name was Jesus, and He died for all of us.

You could hear a pin drop. Every eye was wide and captivated; every ear took in every word. It seemed like the heavens split open, pouring love and comfort upon the grieving people. People embraced what we shared. After our message, the elders asked us to keep singing as people gathered to file past the casket and pay their last respects. We continued to sing until everyone had walked around it and had formed a procession behind it.

The family extended an invitation to us to join everyone at the graveyard, to see an honour tree planted and a beautiful First Nations blanket laid over the casket. I read Psalm 23. Alvina closed in prayer and asked the mourners to repeat the Lord's Prayer. The gang members respectfully removed their hats and joined in repeating the Lord's Prayer.

Alvina and I were invited back to the community centre to fellowship and eat with everyone. Moose nose soup and rabbit stew were among the delicacies expertly prepared. At the end, we were all given a green garbage bag and invited to help ourselves to the leftover fruit, vegetables, and salads or any food we'd like. No one in the village left hungry.

A number of days later, I flew home. I had a three-day turn-around before flying back to Saskatoon to speak at another ladies' conference.

After the conference, I was driven to North Battleford, where I met up with Alvina and Fred. The three of us drove to Edmonton for a national gathering. While there, Alvina and I reconnected with the murdered boy's mother, who lived in Edmonton. She asked us to visit her and said on the phone, "I'll even let you pray with me."

We went to her home the next day. When we walked in, we saw that she had set up a shrine with her son's picture and candles. Beside his picture was my book. She said there was some connection to it, as they had read it to him the night of the wake. We were there for more than an hour listening to her pour out her heart, and before we left, we prayed with her. She hugged us and told us she loved us.

It was a privilege and an honour to be asked by the family to do the service for them. Alvina and I give God all the glory and praise. To this day, we continue to bathe her and the gang members in prayer. We have released all into God's mighty and loving hands.

While on the Thunderchild First Nation Reservation, Alvina and Fred embraced me and treated me royally. They gave me their best, including the use of their master bedroom while they slept in the basement. They wouldn't have it any other way! It was most humbling.

Before I left their home, Fred and Alvina adopted me into their First Nations family. "You are one of us now. You are our sister," they said. "You are now part of our tribe." I was deeply moved.

The following week on our way to Edmonton, Fred and Alvina reminded me again, "You're one of us. You're part of our family." Fred picked up the phone to call his sister who had invited them for dinner to say, "Set an extra place at the table. We're bringing another family member, our sister."

The Edmonton National Gathering was scheduled to open with Indigenous people leading a procession. Alvina and Fred handed me regalia to wear for the grand entry—a ribbon dress and sash. Alvina said, "Belma, put this on. You need to be part of the Grand Entry processional because you're one of us. You're part of our family now."

What a privilege and honour!

Dear heavenly Father, Creator of heaven and earth, thank You for Your tremendous love for these precious people. Thank You for bringing continued comfort and peace to this mother, the gang members and everyone on Thunderchild First Nation. We pray that they would feel You carrying them in Your loving arms. You were there in all the moments of devastation, loss, and grief. Thank You for the way You orchestrated the funeral so that Your hand of love could be extended to each grieving soul. Thank You for giving them grace and strength to walk out this journey with You and with each other and for Your healing oil. We speak blessing over them in Jesus's precious name. Amen.

Chapter 10

Residential Schools

By Alvina Thunderchild

My grandfathers, Chief Morningchild and Chief Thunder-child, are of royal blood. I am the child of a royal blood-line; a royal princess and a queen. My children and their children's children are all royalty. I am a proud citizen of the nation of Thunderchild—but even more so, a proud citizen of heaven, having come from the line of my Father God.

In light of the news of finding the remains of 215 children in Kamloops, so many of my people, including myself, were brought to a traumatic resurfacing and reliving of pain from wrongs done in the past through the residential schools. We remembered the fathers and mothers who were stripped of their parenting positions. There was a great outcry from my nation for justice to be done.

I couldn't help but cry; emotions overwhelmed me. I had to go to my Father God for an answer.

"Lord, what do You have to say about this?" I cried. "Jesus, this was so wrong what happened to our people. Lord, what do You have to say?"

In his tenderness, the Lord spoke and said, "Go read about My people in Exodus."

So I read Exodus 1 to 3.

A new king, to whom Joseph meant nothing, came to power in Egypt. "Look," he said to his people, "the Israelites have become far too numerous for us. Come, we must deal shrewdly with them or they will become even more numerous and, if war breaks out, will join our enemies, fight against us and leave the country."

So they put slave masters over them to oppress them with forced labor ... so the Egyptians came to dread the Israelites and worked them ruthlessly. They made their lives bitter with harsh labor in brick and mortar and with all kinds of work in the fields; in all their harsh labor the Egyptians worked them ruthlessly ...

During that long period, the king of Egypt died. The Israelites groaned in their slavery and cried out, and their cry for help because of their slavery went up to God. God heard their groaning and he remembered his covenant with Abraham, with Isaac and with Jacob. So God looked on the Israelites and was concerned about them ...

The LORD said, "I have indeed seen the misery of my people in Egypt. I have heard them crying out because of their slave drivers, and I am concerned about their suffering. So I have come down to rescue them from the hand of the Egyptians and to bring them up out of that land into a good and spacious land, a land flowing with milk and honey ... The cry of the Israelites has reached me, and I have seen the way the Egyptians are oppressing them. So now, go. I am sending you to Pharaoh to bring my people the Israelites out of Egypt." (Exodus 1:8–14; 2:23–25; 3:7–10)

God has seen and heard the affliction, the groaning, the cries, and the deaths of our people. He was angered by how He was portrayed by the religious people. The enemy, the devil, was like the pharaoh in Exodus. He appointed taskmasters to oppress our people and do away with them. The taskmasters loathed and dreaded our very being. We groaned under their bondage and cried out because of the great oppression and injustice. Jesus describes the enemy: "The thief comes only to steal and kill and destroy; I have come that they may have life, and have it to the full" (John 10:10). The taskmasters stole, killed, and destroyed, but Jesus said, "I have come to give life more *abundantly*."

God heard and God saw. Our God is not an abuser; our God is not a murderer. He is a God of love, and He sent others to break us free from bondage. People were praying for an end of the residential schools, and they came to an end. We are no longer to be under taskmasters that oppress us as they did.

Jesus will heal all the hurts and pains. He has sent *you* and me to proclaim and bring deliverance for our people. *You* have been sent. *You* have that voice. *You* can proclaim, "*I am free from bondage.* I have a right to be healed! I have a right to be free! I have a right to stand and say proudly, 'Yes, the enemy thought he could destroy me, but *my God* saw and heard what was happening. He has sent His Son to deliver me. Now I will go forth and deliver my people.'"

God is for me—not against me. Amen.

[Alvina and Fred Thunderchild are senior pastors of Thunderchild Word Church in Saskatchewan (www.tcwordchurch.com).]

Chapter 11

Visit to Kwadacha and Tsay Keh Dene Communities

By Belma Vardy

Kwadacha

Kwadacha nation is one of the most isolated communities in the Rocky Mountains of northern British Columbia. It is located two hours south of the Yukon and approximately 650 kilometers north of Prince George.

Jeanie Dunbar (a nurse), and her husband Henry (a pastor/carpenter/handyman) have been going to Kwadacha and Tsay Keh Dene, serving the people there since 2005. I was honoured to be travelling with Becky Thomas, a Native American Music Awards recipient as well as a music coach and author, and to serve alongside Jeanie and Henry at these two reservations. Their assistant, Anthony, often took the wheel on the long ten-hour ride up the logging road to these villages. Both Becky and I taught at First Nations Bible College.

Kwadacha Reserve consists of a huge trapping area, with lots of animals and traplines set around many lakes and rivers. Also known as Fort Ware, it was founded as a trading post in the 1920s and was established on the Finley River, close to the confluence of the Fox and Kwadacha rivers. Kwadacha means "white water" in the Tsek'ene language. It has a population of approximately 270 people and is accessed either by plane from Prince George or via rough logging roads. It takes about eight to ten hours to drive from Fort Ware to Prince George, depending on the weather and road conditions.

On this trip, Jeanie, Henry, and Anthony set out the day before Becky and I were to meet each other at the Prince George Airport. They were driving Henry's pickup truck filled with food, props for our activities, and clothing for the people of the villages. As always, they took along extra tires, because tires shred on the primitive logging trails. Becky and I were to sleep at Jeanie and Henry's home and fly the following day to the first village, Kwadacha, on a nine-seater prop plane. We were to meet the three of them there.

When Becky met me at the Prince George Airport, the air was thick with yellow smoke. We couldn't even see across the street. Fires had broken out all across beautiful British Columbia. A yellow-grey fog burned our eyes and lungs. Becky needed medication just to be able to breathe. She had a bad allergy to the air for the first three days and was not well for the first part of the trip. Nevertheless, she soldiered on until her medicine started working

The first thing we did in Prince George was to go to the nearest store. We had planned to teach the children a Hawaiian dance, so we needed costumes. We bought every grass skirt we could find, as well as all the available leis and flowers. We spent most of that night unpacking and repacking since we were allowed to take only twenty-five pounds on the plane the next day.

In the morning I dressed in every stitch of clothing I was taking with me for the two weeks so there would be more room in the suitcase for props and other items. Before we got on the plane, the pilots weighed not only our baggage but us as well, so I stood on the scale. It showed I had gained twenty-seven pounds overnight! We happily anticipated flying north out of Prince George to the village, where the air would be clean and pure.

We practically ran to the plane, covering our faces to try to escape the smoke stinging our eyes and lungs. With the engines throttled and propellers whirling at full speed, we started down the runway, picking up speed and suddenly slowed down. The captain came on: there was a glitch in the engine and we needed to go back. We waited three hours and then got word that we would not be flying out. We had to "come back tomorrow". Oh the disappointment!

Early the next day, we retraced our steps and flew out.

The flight itself was incredible. The farther north we flew, the closer the mountains came together. Twenty minutes before landing, we saw below us the river the plane had been following as a guideline. The pilots maneuvered back and forth between the open spaces of the mountains and through the thickness of B.C.'s wilderness, squeezing the plane between the mountains. The trees looked close enough to touch. Then, suddenly, the plane tipped on its left side in mid-air so dramatically that we felt like we were suddenly lying in bed on our left sides. Barely breathing, we grabbed the seats in front of us to hang on for life while the people in front of us turned to stare at the unruly tourists. We stared back, too terrified to utter a word, our hearts in our throats. Below, the river was at our fingertips!

The pilots were brilliant. We were amazed at their skill during this very challenging leg of the journey and landing. There was no runway. We landed in an opening cleared along the river. That was the first time I experienced a bush pilot's landing. My constitution has improved considerably since then.

We arrived at Kwadacha. Originally the people of Kwadacha were outcasts and outlaws from other tribes, independent of each other. Anyone who couldn't live peaceably with his own tribe was removed from the territory and brought here to live because it was so inaccessible. Everyone in this village had been expelled from their tribe, and no one got along.

It was still the Wild West, reminiscent of the days when British convicts were evicted and sent to Australia's penal colonies. Native people didn't have prisons, so those rejected ended up in this remote "no man's land".

Kwadacha, in the beginning, functioned like a penal colony until eventually descendants bonded. When the government learned of people living there, they started sending in planes to round up the children and take them to residential school. Every Christmas, they returned the children and just dropped them off by the river. One man built a cabin along the river so he could be there when his children got home. Other families did the same and became loosely connected as they waited for their children to come home. Sadly, some of the children never made it home. The ones who did are now the elders.

Even from the air, one can see the depression and poverty that had, at one time, so strongly gripped this village.

At Kwadacha, the chief met and greeted us, warmly welcoming us to his land. We could see children and youth running excitedly with all their dogs (and one wolf) down the mountain and through the thick trees to greet us. What a beautiful sight! Becky had been there before, and they knew her. Every one of them threw their arms around us, giving us great hugs.

I reflected momentarily and took in the scent. How I loved this land—the mountains, trees, rivers, smells of the great outdoors! Since we were so close to the Yukon, I was reminded of the Yukon wilderness and mountains. Breathtaking! Absolutely beautiful!

Within an hour of landing, we were going full steam. The plan was for Becky to teach ukulele classes and me to teach dance. Becky, with the help of Henry and Anthony, started tuning the ukuleles to prepare them for her class. At the same time, I started teaching the children and youth Hawaiian and worship dance on the great, green outdoor carpet of lush grass. Our idea was to teach some of the thirty-eight children to play a certain song on the ukulele to which others would dance, and then together they could do a presentation at the end of the week.

On the first day, Jeanie and Henry drove through the village to make sure every child and every teen was awake and had transportation to the church if needed. They wanted to give them nice, healthy breakfasts to energize them for their ukulele and dance classes. They had brought love offerings of a lot of food. The children started coming on their own after the second meeting. They were hungry and ready to learn!

Jeanie organized a midweek ladies meeting, where she put out a feast, including many baked goods for the women to enjoy. After they ate, I was asked to share my story and lead them into a "God experience". I brought some blue material as a symbolic way of making a river. After I spoke, Becky led the study guide questions, and there was a time of sharing.

One evening, I was asked to lead an "Intimacy with God" workshop in which I encouraged people to engage with their entire beings in physical movement. The presence of the Holy Spirit touched both husbands and wives in a powerful way. Afterward, they had an opportunity to share with all of us about their encounters with the Lord and what He had said to them. Becky and I were so blessed to hear their experiences. As always, Henry and Jeanie provided a delicious feast for all.

There were some days when I took the younger children outside for dancing, singing, and sitting around the unlit firepit. We let the rays of the sun touch us and the wind blow through our hair. As we enjoyed these remote, beautiful outdoor surroundings—God's spectacular creation—some of the children took turns on my lap and I shared Bible stories with them. We danced inside, outside, in the forest, and at the edge of the mountains. Becky led the other group in making crafts and decorating their own ukuleles. Our time together was as memorable for us as it was for them.

During our visit, Becky and I managed to intersperse other activities among the practices. For instance, each time they came,

Jeanie and Henry recorded the names of the children and youth who were baptized. True to tradition, one day we piled all thirty-eight children into vehicles and took them to a place called Sucker Lake, where all the kids and some adults were baptized. After their baptisms, everyone enjoyed a celebratory swim together.

As the practices continued each day, the children and youth came to class more excited than the day before. At the end of the week, they did a presentation of ukulele songs and dances. Sadly, not all of the families were able to come for a variety of reasons. Nevertheless, the children did a fabulous job and had much fun. Their favourite song was a rocky version of "Jesus Loves Me." They screamed and screeched, laughed, and jumped uproariously throughout it. After the presentation, we enjoyed another of Jeanie and Henry's sumptuous feasts.

As our time came to an end, we gifted each of the children with a ukulele and a songbook, Hawaiian grass skirts with leis and flowers and beautiful shawls for the girls, flags for the boys, and T-shirts for all. Becky even gifted a ukulele to one of the fathers of the children so that he and his daughter could play their ukuleles together. We left behind Becky's music CDs and many of my books.

The flags we gave the children were donated by the Ancaster Christian Reformed Church. A group of their ladies purchased material and dowels and set up their sewing machines in the church gym for a sewing weekend. I thank God for Arlene Bennink, who organized this ladies' sewing group.

With many hugs, kisses, and tears, our time together came to an end, and we said our goodbyes. We watched the precious children walk back down the gravel road, through the trees, to their homes, ukuleles on their backs, wearing their shawls, grass skirts and leis, and carrying their flags. It was so hard to watch them go. Our hearts felt broken to part with them.

That evening, Becky and I walked through the reservation, up and down all the pathways and streets, saying goodbye to the land.

Tsay Keh Dene

We then drove seventy kilometres over the bumpy logging road to the next village, the Tsay Keh Dene nation. Tsay Keh Dene village is another very remote, but resilient, community. It, too, is located in the northern region of the Rocky Mountains Trench of northeastern B.C., a valley formed by the eastern and central ranges of the Rockies. Tsay Keh Dene is accessible by a logging road from Mackenzie or by Ootsa Air out of Prince George, B.C.

Our trip to Tsay Keh Dene was somewhat slower than hoped because of elk and a bear crossing in front of us on the logging road. After an hour's drive, we arrived. The people of Tsay Keh Dene are nomadic and have a deep faith in Jesus.

They wander over a very extensive area between Findlay River and the Liard and Nelson rivers. In the spring and fall, they generally return to Fort Graham. Hunter-gatherers do not wander around aimlessly. They have intimate knowledge of their environment and occupy the lands and manage the resources within a bounded territory during their seasonal rounds.

Tsay Keh Dene is a close-knit tribe, and the people are spiritually very powerful. Even though their history shows they've been through a lot, there was a vibrant, cheerful atmosphere evident on this trip. Many homes and trailers were neatly kept. I had the impression that many of the people were genuinely content. They were overjoyed to see us. Many people of Tsay Keh Dene hungrily embraced the Word of God, worship, and prayer. It is their lifeline. Most houses we visited had Bibles. They work hard. They know what all the plants do for different kinds of healing, and they follow the traplines. One thing was for sure: the Lord had made a great difference in their lives and many wholeheartedly acknowledged that fact.

In the 1950s and '60s, the government found the nomadic Tsay Keh Dene people and took all their children away to residential schools. When the kids returned on holidays, they could no longer speak their Sekani language, as they had been made to learn English. They were traumatized, caught between the anger of the school staff if they dared speak Sekani and the anger of their families if they didn't. The parents were devastated at their inability to communicate with their children. Without communication, they could not teach them the survival skills necessary for life. The children lost much of their traditional knowledge related to surviving in their territory and were no longer able to function normally as part of the tribe.

That's when the parents broke down, lost hope, and turned to drinking. They found solace in their addictions. Amazingly, the children all knew Jesus before they went to the residential school and steadfastly kept their relationships with Jesus. The children had been introduced to Him by two teenagers who had met the Sekani in the forest. After receiving Jesus into their hearts, the children were eyewitness to many unusual miracles, some of which are recorded on Becky's *Miracles of the North* CD. The continued occurrence of such miracles served as a plumbline of truth, anchoring the kids in their faith and giving them the ability to discern truth from falsehood, even in the face of a harsh, institutionalized religion. The Jesus they met in the forest had never left them. That's why they were able to have such strong relationships with the Lord coming out of the school; they had known Him before.

In the early '60s, as the tribe was returning from a canoe trip, they turned a bend in their canoes and saw smoke. All five villages of the reservation were on fire. They watched in horror as their villages burned to the ground. One of the girls spotted two people taking off in boats, probably the people who set fire to the villages. All their belongings, rifles, and family pictures were gone. Little did the Sekani people know that, before the perpetrators burnt the cabins, they took everything out of the cabins. No one knew that until years later when they saw all their possessions displayed in the museum in Victoria.

After that, government men arrived with cases of beer and alcohol and got the people drunk. Their plan was to get the tribe to sign a piece of paper to come under certain rules of the government. The Indian agent, at the time, cut them a deal to establish a new reserve and move them to Mackenzie.

Not all agreed, so the tribe was divided. One of the fellows, who was drunk, signed the paper. The officials took his signature as though it was that of the chief and used it to legitimize an agreement with the government to establish a new reserve and move the tribe down to a piece of land at the Mackenzie junction designated as their new reservation. It was close to McLeod Lake and Parsnip River. Their supplies were ferried on riverboats down the Peace River and up the Parsnip to McLeod Lake. A highway was later built connecting the areas. McLeod Lake had a hotel, where the youth would go to get drunk.

The reservation was named Hudson's Bay / Fort Graham Reservation when the government arrived to register everyone and take the kids to residential school. Tsay Keh Dene was on the same side of Williston Lake as Fort Graham. Fort Graham was located between Tsay Keh Dene territory (the other reservation) and the Peace Arm.

After the flooding, as the different tribes made friends, they intermarried and were eventually removed from the original reservation. The government divided them and sent them off to two reservations. All of the Christians ended up in Mackenzie. It wasn't called Tsay Keh Dene at that time.

In 1968, the government ordered B.C. Hydro to build a dam, the WAC Bennett Dam, which formed Williston Lake. The new lake flooded all the hunting ground. Twelve thousand moose got tangled in the debris of the flooding and perished. All five villages in the reservation were underwater, and the forest was very silent. The villages had been burned down so the dam could be built and the people would be out of the way. The people lost their livelihoods, traplines, animals, berry bushes, and hunting and fishing grounds.

The new reservation had no hunting and no fishing. There was nothing available to sustain life. The material for the houses was imported from the States. There was no insulation in them and they were poorly built. Desperate for warmth, the owners would sometimes take their houses apart to burn the wood for fuel. With the young people turning to whiskey and starting to commit crimes, the elders at the new reservation decided to leave. They decided they'd rather die of starvation than lose their children to drugs and alcohol. They were very poor but trusted God for the way ahead. They packed up and moved the people deeper into the mountains.

They kept moving and eventually got so tired that they settled in one spot and built a new village. The new village operated on a family system. Every family was independent, with the senior man in each family making all the decisions. The only problem with the location was that it was very windy. The chief warned against settling there because the excessive wind was not good for their health. However, the tribe didn't listen to him. Now, forty years later, they realize that he was right and are looking to move. The old chief is still alive, but when we were there, his son was chief. Just recently, a new chief was appointed and took over from the old chief's son, who had succeeded him for a time.

In the '90s, B.C. Hydro, showing signs of conscience, built houses for these people. The chief protested that the gesture was not enough reparation for what his people had to go through. In 2009, the people of Tsay Keh Dene finally settled with B.C. Hydro for the damages they suffered due to the creation of the dam. Most chose the settlement in order to move on with their lives, although some felt the settlement was too small.

Previously, some of the tribe members had the opportunity to visit the Victoria Museum when they were enrolling their children in university in Victoria, B.C. To their horror, they saw all their stuff—guns, personal possessions, and pictures from their cabins, which they thought had gone up in smoke. When questioned, they were able to identify all the people in the pictures. The wife of one of the chiefs at the time the kids were being enrolled was the first to find the pictures in Victoria. She tried to initiate an agreement to get the pictures back, but many years of negotiations resulted in only a few photocopies. While they were eventually successful in getting more photocopies, at the time of this writing they are still negotiating with the provincial government regarding their actual belongings and artifacts.

It was these people, who had lost everything to the Bennett Dam and suffered untold other traumas in their lives (like the horrors of residential school), who welcomed us with open arms. They asked us to lead the evening meetings with worship and asked that I share my story. I laid out the blue material and left it as a permanent opportunity for God to continue ministering His healing to them. On their request, we visited people in their homes and prayed for them. Francis, one of the elders, told us he was half blind and couldn't see. He spoke with such sweetness and humility, saying, "God is showing me deep things in the spiritual realm, so I don't have to see the foolish things man is doing."

Because of their deep faith in the Lord, they continue to experience many miracles. With all that these dear people have gone through, they continue to praise the Lord. They say the Creator, in His mercy, heard their cries and pleas for help. As they prayed for more provision, they were answered by Yahweh. They see miracles and supernatural grace over their lives, even today. The heavenly Father, their Healer, hears them when they pray, for the Scriptures promise that whoever calls upon the name of the Lord, Jesus, will be saved. God is their focus in all they do. At one time, this tribe was so full of the Spirit, walking with great favor from God, that Tsay Keh Dene was known to be like heaven on earth.

The Light of Tsay Keh Dene

Tsay Keh Dene was one of the best places to live and raise children before any of these traumatizing events took place. The children once lived wonderful, healthy lives, mostly outdoors; learning about each plant, how to survive, and how to work hard. They could walk for miles. They were a tough people living off the land; running traplines, hunting, fishing, and gathering, moving from camp to camp, depending on what hunting season it was.

On our visit, we gave these people Becky's music CD and my first book, *Because God Was There*.

We were most thankful on this trip to be able to put tools into the hands of the people so they could continue to receive ministry long after we left. The combination of my story and Becky's music would help them worship and heal. It was a joy to be able to leave them behind.

When Henry and Jeanie recently went back to one of the villages, Henry announced that he would be doing baptisms. One mother, who had seven children, five of whom had been baptized, said, "I got two more kids to be baptized, so I will hand them off to you."

Henry said, "No, you won't. I'll baptize your kids tonight, but you've got to stay!" So the mother stayed.

When Henry made the mark of the cross on the first child's forehead, just before baptizing her, a light appeared in front of the child. When the mother saw the glow over the child's head, she gave Henry the second child, and the same thing happened. It happened not only to her children, but to all the other children being baptized as well. When the light appeared in front of each child, the child would start playing with the light. Soon all the children were playing with the light in front of them. The light was an angel.

Soon the adults wanted to get baptized as well. With such a deep faith in God, this village saw many miracles happen in their midst. To this day, miracles are an expected part of life in the village of Tsay Keh Dene.

[Learn more about Becky and her music at www.beckythomas.com and www.hummingbirdcircle.com.]

Chapter 12

"She-Ben-Dum" to "Mod-Zi-Win"

Arlinda (Archi) Buckshot's Story

Boozhoo! Greetings!
My name is Arlinda Buckshot and my Native name is Nokiikwe. It means "Working Woman".

I am of the Pottawatomi lineage and the Bear Clan. My grandmother gave this information to me when I was a little girl of seven years of age. She taught us a lot about the ways of Pottawatomi people, for which I am forever grateful.

I am from Bkejwanong, meaning "Where the Waters Divide". We are known by the Canadian government as the "Walpole Island First Nation #46". We are in unceded territory and were not given this land by the government.

Bkejwanong has always been here, established by the living God Himself. In 1839, the Pottawatomi people arrived and were accepted by the Odawas and the Ojibway tribes. We stayed in the land on the back settlement side, now known as Pottawatomi Island. We are of the Three Fires Confederacy and have coexisted in friendship and peace from that time on.

My seven siblings and I were raised to know the ways of God at an early age. Our parents gave their hearts to the Lord when I was newly born. It is the only way we have known in our spiritual journey. What a rich heritage we have in our family.

I now serve as a senior co-pastor at the Waazhi Kendmowad Church here on Walpole Island. We have "she-ben-dum" (boldness) to "mod-zi-win" (speak life), to bring the good news of the gospel of Jesus, the Son of God.

My sister, Karen, and I are on our local radio station, CFRZ, at 98.3 FM, every morning, five days a week, from seven to eight a.m., for a full hour of gospel tunes and exhortation from the Bible. Since the pandemic came, our church has been the local radio for "radio church" on Sunday mornings from nine to ten a.m. We are also online, so that the northern tribes can catch the messages of hope.

The website is www.walpoleislandfirstnation.ca. If you click on the community link and wait a bit, you'll be in. God bless you as you listen.

On another note, I wish to express my feelings directly to the residential school survivors: As innocent, young children, you were robbed of your childhood. You were stolen away to be assimilated into the dominant culture of that era. I just want you to know that two thousand years ago, Jesus saw the injustice that would be done to you, and He did something about it. He bought you with a priceless gift, the gift of His own blood. He was born into this world of humanity because God loves people of every race, creed, and colour. This includes Native populations. All you have to do now is reach out to Him, and He will look after you in heaven through all eternity.

Regarding the children who are being found in unmarked graves, those children are very much alive! All those little spirits went home to be with Jesus.

In June 2021, when the bodies of precious children were being found in unmarked graves in Kamloops, near the Kamloops Residential School, the living God spoke a word through me to Canada. This is what was spoken:

"The living God speaks this Word to you. I have called the nation of Canada to repentance. I have witnessed the deaths of My innocent children caused by the government's founding fathers. These little ones' blood was spilled and hidden for a century. It has cried out to Me. I have gathered My little children onto Myself. They move and live in My heavenly kingdom. The loss of My little ones left fractured and sad families. Do not cry and mourn anymore for them. My people—do not carry this burden any longer, for your loved ones are with Me, and they have rest in Me. They have rest in Me."

In 1875, Bishop Vital Grandin declared that the goal of the residential school program was to instill a pronounced distaste for Native life in the children, so they would feel humiliated when reminded of their origins. He promised that upon graduation from the schools, the children would have lost everything Native except their blood.

But he didn't understand. Life is in the blood. Our Native identity is in our DNA. They tried to change us from the outside, but they could not change us on the inside.

We've been here for thousands of years. We've survived sickness, pandemic, and residential schools. God has brought us through a lot. We're here because God has a plan for our lives. God knew each of us before we were born, and He gave each of us a special gift to make a difference in the world. He's still with us now through His Holy Spirit. He's taking care of us because He loves us so much.

There's a common ground in our message. We don't know each other from different territories, but no matter what comes our way, we choose to swim and not sink and hold our heads up high. We're still here. We're still strong. We must thank the Creator every day we get up. His breath is in our lungs. His strength is in our bones.

From our knowledge of the earthly journey of the short life of Jesus Christ, we natives have learned that we are special to God. We have been keepers of the land and of the waters so that there will be something left for the generations to come.

Christ brought the black book, the Bible, the Truth of God, to us too. What we learn from the Bible makes our lives more peaceful and happier, knowing that God has everything under control.

To each of you, I say, "Don't give up, God loves you and cares for you like no other father can. He truly loves you and has brought you through scary years of your early life. He is still waiting for you to talk to Him and praise Him for His goodness."

Pray the following prayer to accept what the Lord and Saviour Jesus did for you and me. Give God a chance; He is waiting to hear from you.

"Heavenly Father God, I ask for forgiveness for my sins. I ask Jesus to come into my heart and wash me clean. Help me to follow You all the days of my life. I look forward to my eternal home in heaven with Jesus. Chii-miigwech."

God Is Present
Springtime Is Muskrat Time
By Arlinda Buckshot

Through all our times of survival God is with us in everything we do! April is here and the sounds of the redwing blackbirds and the robins prompt my memories of when Dad would be preparing for his annual trapline. Those particular birds always signalled that spring had arrived along with them. As we watched the ice floes coming down the Snye channel, Dad always had his trap sticks cut and tagged. He often maintained his coney bear and stop-loss traps over the long winter months. He made sure his gear was waterproofed and patched if needed. He even built his punt paddles and boat in the living room of the house!

I thought everyone did this but afterward found out that wasn't true for every household on the island. Dad also liked to make his own "minnows" for ice fishing in the winter. This carving took place in the house too. There were always wood shavings to sweep up.

Dad would set off in the morning and would often stay down the lake for a few days at a time. This would allow him to have valuable time to skin the muskrats he'd catch. Many times, he brought the skinned hides home to Mom and she'd stretch them. She was a genuine "super mom"!

As we children got a little older, Dad would bring his catch home every night. We'd sit in a circle in the kitchen and skin muskrats and dry the wet hides and then stretch them. Jeff, Kevin, Karen, and I would skin, and Patsy and Mom would stretch the hides. We had an assembly line happening until the midnight hour. It is a wonder any of us kids graduated from school. Then we had to haul the meat away and save some of it for a good supper later on. No one could cook those muskrats like Mom could. I believe that she inherited her cooking prowess from Grandma Bernice.

There was a lot of excitement when we would hear the hum of Dad's outboard coming down the Blue Water Conference. We'd race down to the riverbank and grab the rope to get his boat tied securely. The hard part was lugging all the catch of the day to the kitchen floor for "processing".

Many times, the muskrats were in burlap bags and the boys would tag-team to get those heavy loads to the house. It was quite a walk for kids to manage. Often, my cousin Conrad was there to help Uncle Jr. and Aunt Connie with the skinning of hides. Dad would pay piecework to whoever helped. Our own immediate family did it as part of family survival. It was all part of putting food in the cupboard and clothes on our backs. I remember best the camaraderie that we kids felt as we busily skinned and talked about everything under the sun.

Our house smelled of raw hides drying—a smell I have never forgotten. I guess we became used to that smell. Dad said it was the "smell of money". We girls wondered if we smelled like drying muskrat hides when we went to school. It saturated the house. Nothing escaped its clutches! We were always grabbing our perfume. The payoff was good because that meant the bills could get paid and there would be good food in the cupboards. We usually got to pick out something we needed for ourselves. Usually that meant clothes, maybe a new jacket. We felt a sense of accomplishment because we kids worked to contribute to the betterment of the family income. We loved our parents and wanted to assist in any way we were able. They, in turn, taught us that through hard work and perseverance, we could accomplish anything.

The fur buyer would come by and sort the hides into sizes. He would look over each dry hide and feel the thickness. Then he would give dad a price per hide. Sometimes, in good times, it would reach as high as eight dollars each. But I also remember the price plummeting down to two dollars each. When times were good, Dad would sell the hides and easily get $3,500 for his batch of hides. We kids would stand off to the side and watch this pan of bartering and keep very quiet. I guess we were in suspense to see so much money at one time and how much would remain in our house.

This was a big part of living in a home where our father was a hunter/ trapper/ fisherman. I would not have traded it for anything else in the world. Dad was good at everything having to do with wildlife and many times we ate wild meats and foods. We ate muskrat and whatever was in season.

I know those days are gone and will probably never be lived as before, but I feel that many people in their community that are in the same age proximity will remember those days. It wasn't too far off. Cherish those memories and tell the children and grandchildren. Keep those times alive, no matter how insignificant they may seem. It is how we survived as a nation. God was there!

RECIPE: SMOTHERED MUSKRAT AND ONIONS

1 Muskrat
1 tbsp. salt
1 quart water
1½ tsp. salt
¼ tsp. paprika
1½cups flour
3 tbsp. fat
3 large onions, sliced
1 cup sour cream

Skin and clean the muskrat; remove fat, scent glands and white tissue inside each leg.

Soak the muskrat overnight in a weak brine solution of 1 tbsp. salt to 1 glass of water.

Drain, disjoint and cut up.

Put flour, salt and paprika in a paper bag.

Add muskrat pieces and shake until each piece is well-coated.

Melt fat in heavy fry pan, add the muskrat pieces and sauté slowly until browned.

When meat is browned, cover with onions, sprinkle with salt and pepper and pour the cream over. Cover fry pan and simmer for 1 hour.

Yield: 4 servings

Chapter 13

"Goh-Waub-Min"

By Arlinda Buckshot

I was talking with an old friend the other day about long- ago stuff. Life was so much simpler and less stressful. There was a time when we didn't have the media, such as it is today, to add to the calamity of our community. When we needed to go somewhere, like to the store or to school, we had to walk there.

Laundry was done at home with a tub of water and wash-boards. My sister Karen and I always washed clothing and diapers by hand on the scrub board to help Mom out and do our part to take the load of running a large household off of her shoulders. I thought we were among the elite when Dad bought a wringer washer! He would take it outside in the summer and place it next to a hydro pole, by the fish pond, down on the Snye channel. He would plug it into the power box and we thought it couldn't get any better than that! All we had to do was get a pail and pour water into the tub and the clothes would wash themselves. Another wash tub was set down next to it for rinse water. We very carefully passed the wet, rinsed clothes through the rubber rollers, and all we had to do then was hang them on the line! What a marvellous invention! The novelty soon wore off though.

Mom also got a little floor polisher/ scrubber machine to make our floors shiny clean. We got a vacuum cleaner soon after and there were lots of ways that we found it to be useful. One time, our parents went to the mainland to shop. Because of the little six-car ferry that was the only way for vehicles to come and go from the island, it would take about three to four hours to conduct business and make it home. We kids knew we could count on them being away for at least that stretch of time.

Being the procrastinators we were when we had chores to do, Jeff and Karen decided to make life one step easier. They had an idea that we would use the vacuum to dry all the dishes that were supposed to be done by the time our parents came home. Well, you can probably guess—it did not work out that way at all. When the wet dishes were all spread out on the table on dish towels and the vacuum was turned on, the bad idea became instantly apparent. Jeff forgot about all the dirt that was contained in the vacuum when he reversed the airflow! How awful when we saw all the dirt being blown out on all those dishes; not only on the dishes, but on the kitchen floor and on us! We had an instant dust storm in Mom's kitchen.

All I could think was that they'd be home in maybe half-an-hour and there'd be big trouble if the house looked like that. So we swung into crisis mode and every able-bodied Lallean kid took action to clean up. Miracle of miracles, we had the house tidied up in nothing flat. It is amazing what you can do with a little motivation—namely, the threat of a willow switch treatment if the house was a mess!

Karen came up with some unique ways to help too. Our mom was the hairstylist and barber at our house. She had a set of barber scissors and electric-powered hair clippers. Karen decided she was going to cut Kevin's hair. It was summertime, and school was fast approaching. Jeff wanted to help Karen, so they tag-teamed poor Kevin's crowning glory. When they finished with his hair, he took a look and found a stocking hat to cover his head. Mom and Dad came home and didn't immediately notice the hat on his head. As it was a hot summer day, they began to have a sneaking suspicion that something wasn't right. Off came his hat and out came his confession! Karen and Jeff were scolded for touching Mom's barbershop items.

Karen was always making life interesting for everyone in her little circle and territory. She is still doing the same today, in much different ways! Well—you have got to hear this story of when Karen first entered into "ministry".

We had an uncle named Virgil, who was married to our aunt Charlene. He raised pigs on the Lallean property for a few years during our young lives on Soney Road. One day, Jeff and Karen came upon a drowned piglet in a ditch near the house we lived in. They immediately told Uncle Virgil and he checked out the situation and said, "It's dead, all right." Then he told Jeff and Karen to bury it.

They took the piglet and dug a grave for it near Gram's log house. Karen picked some weeds for flowers for the funeral of this poor drowned piglet. Jeff put the pig in the ground and covered it up with dirt. He then told Karen to say a prayer before she put the flowers on the grave. Karen began to say the Lord's Prayer and Jeff told her, "Not that way—pray like Oral Roberts prays!" So Karen then prayed, "In the name of Jesus," and then stuck those hard weeds into the grave of that piglet. Immediately, that little pig shot up out of that shallow grave and took off running! Thus began the days of Karen's ministry! And I'd like to add that Karen is a woman of great faith today. That gal knows how to pray.

I'd like to encourage anyone who needs encouraging. You may have circumstances and situations that look bleak. You may think that no one cares—but we do care and so does the great Creator. He can lift your heart out of depression and put a song in its place. Keep on walking strong in your earth walk and never forget to thank the One who has provided for First Nations people in all aspects of our lives down through the years. Just like a commercial we saw on television, "No problem too big! No problem too small! Father and Son ... they do it all! Until next time my friends ...."

Goh waub min ("I'll see you later" in Ojibway).

Chapter 14

God Heard and Came Running

Karen Lallean's Story

L et me say something about myself.

I am Arlinda's sister, a Native girl. I have lived on Walpole Island most of my life. The island sits between Ontario, Canada, and Michigan, USA, at the mouth of the St. Clair River. It's been home to Aboriginal people for thousands of years, and about 2,000 Ojibway, Pottawatomi, and Ottawa live here now. It was a wonderful place to grow up, despite the sense of hopelessness that remains with many of our people after their experiences in the residential schools. With about twenty-six square miles of the richest and most varied wetlands in all of the lands of the Great Lakes, home to lots of rare plants and abundant wildlife, we still support our families through hunting, fishing, trapping, and guiding work.

I come from a family of eight kids; four girls and four boys. We were blessed with wonderful, parents. My parents always took us to church and gave us direction about how to live our lives; but most of all, they were great role models for us as children. They gave us an understanding of life and how to live it. We have a priceless heritage that has helped us to live with strength, direction and purpose.

Now I teach my nieces and nephews—and anyone else who will listen—about the words and the ways we were taught. These simple words of encouragement will never leave me—like, "Don't make fun of people because you might have a child someday, and maybe they might have problems." My dad would tell us, "Don't fight with your brothers and sisters. They might be the only friends you'll have." I listened to them and am thankful for their wisdom.

One thing Dad told me was, "Karen, you have a brain; use it. If someone was jumping off a building, would you jump too?" I had a learning disability and couldn't read. I failed grade 2 and grade 5. I didn't even go to grade 8, but I got sent to a grade 9 special education class. Instead of giving up on me, Dad encouraged me to be strong.

One day when I was fourteen years old, in total desperation, I cried out to Jesus to help me read so I could understand what was put in front of me. God heard and came running to help me. Everything changed after that moment. I remember being suddenly aware of the birds singing beautifully and the breeze blowing like the breath of God on my face. I felt the love of God so clearly. Right then, I asked Jesus to come into my life and forgive me of my sins. I'll never forget that day. He's been with me ever since.

I was raised on the reservation (or "the rez" as we say). My grandma, my dad's mom, was a very special lady to me; she always talked about the Lord Jesus to us. When we were kids, we would go and stay with her. She was crippled from very painful arthritis. Her hands were gnarled out of shape. She found it difficult to hold anything or do simple things. She was in bed and couldn't get up, but I loved her dearly. My brother Jeff and my sister Arlinda and I would stay with her. We lived next door in the old log house. I would comb her long, grey hair and learned how to braid it and wash her up. It was at Grandma's that I learned how to cook on a wood stove. The pots would be black on the bottom from cooking, so she would tell me to empty the ashes and take those pots outside and rub them in the ashes to get the soot off them. I'd scrub and rub those pots until the soot was totally gone and they shone. Those ashes worked every time.

My relationship with God is real and makes a difference in the way I live every day. It's not just a religion that puts me in a box of rules. My faith is a gift that helps me live my life with strength and confidence—but I know I have to do my part to make it happen the way God intended. Ephesians 4:32 says I have been forgiven, so I forgive others whenever I feel bad things have been said or done to me. Ephesians 2:14 says that through Christ I have access by one Spirit to the Father. In other words, I have a direct line to Jesus and I make sure I use it.

I have been an addictions worker for almost thirty years in my community on Walpole Island. There's a huge problem here with the trafficking and use of illegal substances leading to suicides and opioid overdoses. I feel God's heart for my people and long to help them understand His love for them. They need to know they're not alone and people care about them. They need hope.

For my education, I attended George Brown College in Toronto and trained as a worker in a day-care. Then, I went to Lambton College in Brocket, Alberta, for a year to become a teacher for a children's centre. Later on, I went to St. Clair College to take an addictions course for two years.

Throughout the years, I always wanted to be a radio DJ; so for the past twenty-four years, I have been doing the "Karen in the Morning Show" on CFRZ 98.3 FM. Now it is broadcast all over the place on the internet and my desire has come true. I feel like God put this dream in my heart as a way to reach more people than I could have ever thought possible.

Although I have lived a full life, it hasn't always been roses. I've had three bouts of cancer and presently am going through chemotherapy. Yet I know I'll get through this with the grace of God. His mercy is new every morning and His grace is enough for me.

I want to shine as a light to the world. Philippians 2:14–16 states, "Do everything without grumbling or arguing, so that you may become blameless and pure, 'children of God without fault in a warped and crooked generation.' Then you will shine among them like stars in the sky as you hold firmly to the word of life."

So take heart people. Don't let life get you down. You have a hope in Jesus.

God bless you.

Chapter 15

The Big Steel Doors

Belma Vardy's
Concluding Words

Despite the fact that I do not have First Nations blood running through my veins, my love for the people of the land runs strong in my heart. While our nationalities differ, our shared experiences run deep. That's why our hearts are bonded.

My father was born in Yugoslavia. His father, my grandfather, was one of the richest men in the country. He owned hotels, banks, restaurants, and a lot of land. It was a wonderful family until Communism reared its ugly head and destroyed everything that was once beautiful. Soldiers kidnapped my grandfather, took all his money and possessions, and threw him in jail. My father—his son—was unable to help him and fled north to Austria. My grandmother fled south with my father's two sisters to Turkey. As among the First Nations people, where a foreign ideology took over the land and the children were taken to residential schools, our family was torn apart by invaders. It was nineteen years before my father saw his family again.

After I was born, his dream was to fly to Turkey with my mother and me to introduce us to his parents and family. My mother, who had tried three times to abort me before I was born, made it clear that she did not want to go there. "I'll go to China; I'll go to Africa—but I will never go with you to Turkey," she said. It ripped my father apart not to be able to take his beloved daughter to meet his precious relatives, especially his parents.

His dream became mixed with his memories and I remember him describing to me the big steel doors at the Istanbul airport. Eyes brimming with tears, he told me how his beautiful family would be waiting on the other side. He imagined how the doors would open and he would carry me through them in his arms, to present me to his family. Over and over throughout the years, he shared this dream with me. When both his parents (my grand-parents) passed, it was shattered.

In 2004, when I was an adult, my father went to Turkey, and we planned for me to travel there to meet all my relatives. So there I was—landing in Turkey for the first time.

After picking up my suitcases, I walked to the door that took me to the main hall where my father and relatives were waiting to greet me.

I was full of emotion and excited to see him, fully anticipating meeting everyone. Luggage in hand, I walked down a hall and around a corner. Suddenly, there in front of me were the big steel doors. Shiny and silver, they stretched from ceiling to floor. Tears streamed down my face as the memory of my father's lost dream overwhelmed my senses. I remembered his hope of carrying me, presenting me. Sadness fell over me at the memory of his pain. But then a voice said, "And now I, your heavenly Father, will carry you through these doors." I felt His breath impart strength and His loving hands scoop me up. A gentle peace flowed through me. I took a step.

Is there a door in your life that needs to be opened?

Do you need to be carried through it?

You are not walking through those doors alone. His presence is ever surrounding you. God promises never to leave us or forsake us.

The Lord says to you: "Do not fear, for I am with you; do not be dismayed, for I am your God. I will strengthen you and help you; I will uphold you with my righteous right hand" (Isaiah 41:10). "Be strong and courageous. Do not be afraid; do not be discouraged, for the LORD your God will be with you wherever you go" (Joshua 1:9).

Now as I reflect on my dad telling me, time after time, about his dream, I understand that the steel doors represent his love for me and the pride he felt at the thought of being able to present me to his family, but Mother stopped that from happening. His hope was smashed, removed, ripped out from under him, and destroyed—forever shattered.

I thought of my Indigenous brothers and sisters—the times I've had living with them, and seeing their hopes and dreams constantly shattered—promise after promise unfulfilled, withdrawn, stripped, and destroyed.

Native culture is beautiful. I'm in love with it and with the people. The depth of worship that I have experienced among Native people who know their Creator in a personal way is one I have never encountered elsewhere. It radiates beauty and a peace through harmony with God's creation.

Jesus loves Indigenous people. He is a God of love, kindness, peace, mercy, and grace. It is so grievous how He has been misrepresented to Native people through most residential schools, churches, and society. These institutions have not presented the First Nations people with the true nature of God, our heavenly Father, whose heart cry is to carry us through doors from oppression into freedom and into a welcoming community. He created the Indigenous people with amazing abilities and a unique identity to adapt and survive in an often harsh land. He has a plan for their lives, and I believe He has "reserved" them for such a time as this.

In this book you've had the eye-opening privilege of seeing into the incredible lives of some very special people. Each has shared raw details of their personal struggles as they have found their way from the slippery, craggy paths of pain and sorrow, onto life-giving open spaces of restoration and healing.

Regardless of how harsh the circumstances, transformation was only possible *because the Spirit was there.*

May God, our heavenly Father, bring the Indigenous people into a glorious place of honour as the unique people He created them to be, and may their culture be embraced and treasured. May any steel doors shut before them be opened for God's unending blessings to pour into their lives for generations to come, and may His Glory descend upon them.

About the Author

Belma Vardy is a Bible college graduate, author of *Because God Was There*, and an ordained minister with Global Christian Ministry Forum. She was born in Toronto, Canada, and raised in Berlin, Germany, by her grandparents. Belma lives in Ontario, Canada, the home base for her Celebration of Dance ministry.

From 1995, Belma has worked closely with leaders and elders in the Inuit, Metis, and First Nations communities to bring a ministry of freedom through artistic expression of their culture and rich heritage. Belma has been embraced by First Nations as "part of this family, our tribe, our sister". She considers it a tremendous privilege to receive many eagle feathers from various chiefs—one of the highest honours in their culture.

For thirty-four years, Belma has ministered in dance and therapeutic movement to people with gentleness and dedication, leading them into deeper intimacy and freedom with the Creator. Her ministry is a vessel for bringing God's power into people's lives, resulting in testimonies of inner healing, deep experiences of the Father's love, and new levels of freedom in worship. Under the guidance of the Holy Spirit, she produced many worship dance videos/ DVDs for children, youth, and adults. Due to her special love for children, she was appointed coordinator for the International Christian Dance Fellowship's (ICDF) Network for Children's Dance. Belma also served for seven years as the national coordinator, representing Canada for adult worship dance, with the Christian Dance Fellowship of Canada, under the umbrella of ICDF.

A seasoned public speaker and workshop leader, she has taught and presented throughout Canada, the United States, Europe, South Africa, Asia, the United Kingdom, South America, the Caribbean Islands, and the Arctic.

Belma has made guest appearances on *100 Huntley Street*, *Circle Square Discovery*, *Miracle Channel*, and *Catch the Fire* (television shows and radio programs). Her testimony is published in Dr. Guy Chevreau's *Catch the Fire* and *Pray with Fire*.

In her first book, *Because God Was There*, Belma shares her amazing testimony of loss, healing, and overcoming. She also has a podcast "Heavenly Interventions by Belma Vardy".

Belma's books and other projects are under the covering of Imago (www.imago-arts.on.ca). All who wish to make tax-deductible donations toward the production, translation, and distribution of her books and other projects can make cheques payable to "The Freedom Project" and forward them to Belma Vardy, P.O. Box 20104, 2211 Brant St., Burlington, Ontario, Canada L7P 0A4; or send an e-transfer to belmavardy@celebrationofdance.com.

For More Information

Connect with Belma Vardy

Learn more about Belma's ministry and how you can experience genuine healing and freedom through the love of God. Discover all that her ministry has to offer through invaluable resources online, or connect with Belma to book a speaking engagement for your group.

CONTACT

Phone
905-336-1499

Email
belmavardy@celebrationofdance.com

Address
P.O. Box 20104, 2211 Brant St.,
Burlington, Ontario, Canada L7P 0A4

Facebook
@belmavardytravels

To book a speaking engagement, order resources, or learn more about Belma's ministry, please visit

www.celebrationofdance.com

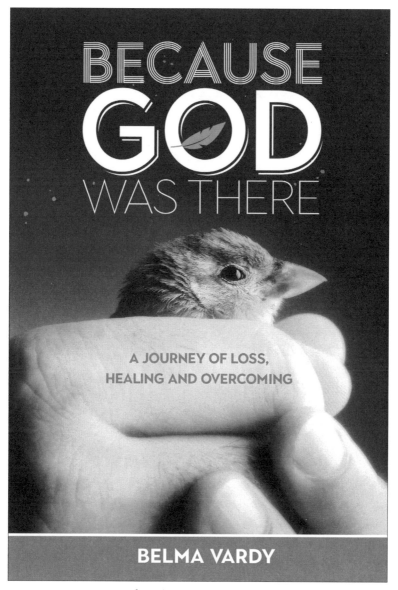

BECAUSE
GOD
WAS THERE

A JOURNEY OF LOSS,
HEALING AND OVERCOMING

BELMA VARDY

CASTLE QUAY BOOKS

OTHER TITLES BY CASTLE QUAY BOOKS

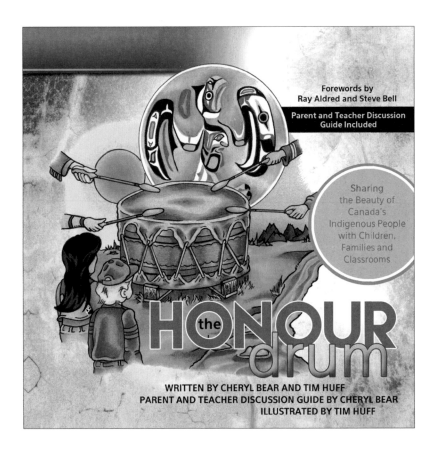

OTHER TITLES BY CASTLE QUAY BOOKS

OTHER TITLES BY CASTLE QUAY BOOKS

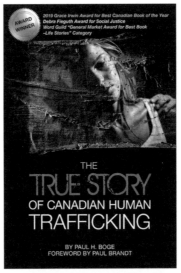

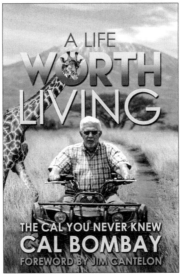

OTHER TITLES BY CASTLE QUAY BOOKS